T0283625

THE DANUBE CYCLEWAY VOLUME 2

FROM BUDAPEST TO THE BLACK SEA

by Mike Wells

JUNIPER HOUSE, MURLEY MOSS,
OXENHOLME ROAD, KENDAL, CUMBRIA LA9 7RL
www.cicerone.co.uk

© Mike Wells 2023
Second edition 2023
ISBN: 978 1 78631 189 4
First edition 2016

Printed in Singapore by KHL Printing on responsibly sourced paper.
A catalogue record for this book is available from the British Library.
All photographs are by the author unless otherwise stated.

Route mapping by Lovell Johns www.lovelljohns.com
Contains OpenStreetMap.org data © OpenStreetMap contributors, CC-BY-SA.
NASA relief data courtesy of ESRI

Updates to this Guide

While every effort is made by our authors to ensure the accuracy of guide-books as they go to print, changes can occur during the lifetime of an edition. Any updates that we know of for this guide will be on the Cicerone website (www.cicerone.co.uk/1189/updates), so please check before planning your trip. We also advise that you check information about such things as transport, accommodation and shops locally. Even rights of way can be altered over time.

The route maps in this guide are derived from publicly available data, databases and crowd-sourced data. As such they have not been through the detailed checking procedures that would generally be applied to a published map from an official mapping agency, although naturally we have reviewed them closely in the light of local knowledge as part of the preparation of this guide.

We are always grateful for information about any discrepancies between a guidebook and the facts on the ground, sent by email to updates@cicerone.co.uk or by post to Cicerone, Juniper House, Murley Moss, Oxenholme Road, Kendal LA9 7RL.

Register your book: To sign up to receive free updates, special offers and GPX files where available, create a Cicerone account and register your purchase via the 'My Account' tab at www.cicerone.co.uk.

Front cover: Golubacki grad castle (Stage 15) guards the entrance to the Iron Gates gorge (photo by loan/stock.adobe.com)

CONTENTS

Kalocsa cathedral in baroque style (Stage 3)

ROUTE SUMMARY TABLE

Stage	Start	Finish
1	Budapest, chain bridge	Ráckeve, Árpád bridge
2	Ráckeve, Árpád bridge	Solt, Béke tér square
3	Solt, Béke tér square	Foktő
4	Foktő	Baja, Szentháromság tér square
5	Baja, Szentháromság tér square	Mohács, ferry ramp
6	Mohács, ferry ramp	Osijek, Pješački bridge
7	Osijek, Pješački bridge	Vukovar, Vuka bridge
8	Vukovar, Vuka bridge	Bačka Palanka, St John the Baptist churc
9	Bačka Palanka, St John the Baptist church	Novi Sad, Varadinski bridge
10	Novi Sad, Varadinski bridge	Novi Slankamen, crossroads
11	Novi Slankamen, crossroads	Belgrade, St Alexander Nevsky church
12	Belgrade, St Alexander Nevsky church	Kovin, marina
13	Kovin, marina	Stara Palanka, ferry ramp
14	Stara Palanka, ferry ramp	Golubac, main square
15	Golubac, main square	Donji Milanovac, tourist office
16	Donji Milanovac, tourist office	Drobeta-Turnu Severin, Tudor park
17	Drobeta-Turnu Severin, Tudor park	Gruia, church
18	Gruia, church	Calafat, town hall
19	Calafat, town hall	Bechet, Dn55 junction
20	Bechet, Dn55 junction	Corabia, post office
21	Corabia, post office	Turnu Măgurele, central park
22	Turnu Măgurele, central park	Zimnicea, town hall
23	Zimnicea, town hall	Giurgiu, Turkish watchtower
24	Giurgiu, Turkish watchtower	Oltenița, central park
25	Oltenița, central park	Călăraşi, Volna church
26	Călăraşi, Volna church	Ion Corvin, Dj223 junction
27	Ion Corvin, Dj223 junction	Cernavodă, roundabout
28	Cernavodă, roundabout	Hârşova, Dn22a junction
29	Hârşova, Dn22a junction	Măcin, Dn22 junction
30	Măcin, Dn22 junction	Galați, ferry ramp
31	Galați, ferry ramp	Isaccea, mosque
32	Isaccea, mosque	Tulcea, Oraş station
Total km		
Variant		
27–32	Ion Corvin, Dj223 junction	Tulcea, Oraş station
Total km		
31A	Galați, ferry ramp	Isaccea, mosque
32A	Tulcea, quayside	Sulina, Black Sea beach

Distance	Waymarking	Page
47km	EV6	44
50.5km	EV6	54
40.5km	EV6	60
44.5km	EV6	65
34km	EV6	70
81km; alt route 84.5km	EV6, then Ruta Dunav	75
44.5km	Ruta Dunav EV6	84
40.5km	Ruta Dunav EV6	89
43.5km	Dunavska ruta EV6	94
41km	Dunavska ruta EV6	99
53km	Dunavska ruta EV6	105
67km; alt route 56.5km	Dunavska ruta EV6	114
39.5km; alt route 40km	Dunavska ruta EV6	122
38km	Dunavska ruta EV6	125
57km	Dunavska ruta EV6	129
67km	Dunavska ruta EV6	135
71.5km	follow Dn6, Dn56a, Dn56b, Dn56c	144
62.5km	follow Dn56c, Dn56a, Dn56	149
96km	follow Dn55a	154
45.5km	follow Dn54a	161
30.5km	follow Dn54	165
57km	follow Dn51a	168
60km	follow Dn5c	172
76km	follow Dn5, Dn41	178
70km	follow Dn31	184
65km	follow Dn3	190
40.5km	follow Dj223	196
53km	follow Dj223	201
88km	follow Dj222f, Dn22d	206
30km	follow Dn22, Dn22b	211
42km	follow Dn22e, Dn22	217
36km	follow Dn22	227
1712km		
223km	follow Dn3, Dc86, Dj226, Dj222	235
1646km		
52km	via Ukraine	221
147km round trip	by boat	232

The Liberty monument in Budapest was originally
the Russian victory monument (Stage 1)

INTRODUCTION

The chain bridge spans the Danube between Buda (left) and Pest (right) (Stage 1)

The upper and middle Danube from Germany through Austria to Vienna and on to Budapest in Hungary is one of the world's most popular cycle routes, followed by cyclists of all ages and abilities. (For a description of the route from the Black Forest to Budapest see *The Danube Cycleway Volume 1* by the same author.) But the Danube Cycleway does not end at Budapest. It continues for another 1712km at first through Hungary, then the countries of Croatia and Serbia (former Yugoslavia) and Romania, all the way to the Black Sea. The cycleway still follows the river, but the resemblance ends there. Unlike the well-developed tourist infrastructure of Germany and Austria, after Budapest you enter a region where tourism is still in its infancy.

As a result, by cycling the lower Danube you embark upon an adventure where the very journey becomes something of a challenge. Tourist offices, places to stay and cycle shops are few and far between, while West European languages are little spoken. You need to plan accommodation ahead and be more self-sufficient when it comes to maintaining your cycle in working order. The fact that you cross the line of the former Iron Curtain twice, pass through an area that was involved in a violent civil war as recently as 1999 and skirt the edge of the old Soviet Union all add to the sense of adventure. But don't be discouraged by this. Cycling the lower Danube is well within the capabilities of most cycle tourists. The people are warm and friendly and both road surfaces and waymarking have improved a lot in recent years. This book is intended to help the average cyclist complete this adventure successfully.

The 2772km-long Danube is Europe's second longest river (behind the Volga). Rising in the German Black Forest, it runs through 10 countries on its way to the Black Sea. This guidebook covers the 1647km that the river flows from Budapest to the extensive delta in Romania where it empties into the sea. As the Danube has dropped to an altitude of only 100m above sea level by the time it reaches Budapest, the cycleway following the river is mostly level. Through Hungary and Serbia the route follows long off-road stretches along flood dykes. In Romania cycling is mostly along the Romanian Danube road (Strada Dunarii), a quiet long-distance road set back from the river alongside the flood plain, which was built in the mid-19th century to open up the southern part of the newly unified country.

The route follows part of EuroVelo route 6 (EV6), a trans-continental cycle route running from the Atlantic coast of France to the Black Sea. This is well waymarked in Hungary and Serbia, partly so in Croatia but unmarked in Romania. This guide breaks the route into 32 stages, averaging 53.5km per stage. In theory a fit cyclist covering 90km per day should be able to complete the trip in 19 days. However, this is difficult to achieve because of unequal distances between overnight accommodation, and so, unless you are camping, it is advisable to plan on taking between three and four weeks.

The main sights encountered en route include the great cities of Budapest and Belgrade and the rugged Iron Gates gorges where the Danube has forced its way through a gap between the Carpathian and Balkan mountain ranges. Although the river rushing through the gorge has been tamed by the construction of two huge dams, this is still an awe-inspiring place. The lake behind the dams has flooded Roman Emperor Trajan's military road that followed the river and a new corniche road has been built which climbs above the gorge with spectacular views. The route ends in the Danube Delta, Europe's largest area of natural wetland and home to an enormous variety of bird species. Although the cyclable route ends 73km short of the river mouth, it is possible (and recommended) to take a boat through the delta to the zero kilometre point where the Danube enters the Black Sea, a suitable place to conclude your adventure at the very end of Europe.

BACKGROUND

As the major river of central and south-eastern Europe, the Danube has played significant roles in the history of the continent, first as a border, then as an invasion route and later as an important transport and trade artery.

A reconstruction of a section of Trajan's Roman bridge over the Danube in Drobeta-Turnu Severin (Stage 16)

A Roman frontier

The first civilisation to recognise the importance of the river was the Romans. After pushing north through the Balkans, they arrived on the banks of the lower Danube around 9BC. Seeing the value of a natural and defendable northern border to protect their empire from barbarian tribes, the Romans established fortified settlements along the river from Germany all the way to the Black Sea, the largest of these in the section covered by this guide being Aquincum (near Budapest), Singidunum (Belgrade), Viminacium (near Kostolac) and Durostorum (Silistra). The Romans knew the border area as the Limes and settlements were connected by a series of military roads. The Romans advanced across the Danube (AD101) into Dacia (modern day Romania) but withdrew again in AD271. After the Roman Empire split in two (AD330), the province of Pannonia (modern day Hungary and Croatia) became part of the Western Empire and Moesia (Bulgaria and Serbia) part of the Eastern (later Byzantine) Empire. The Western Roman Empire collapsed and was overrun by barbarians in the fifth century, leaving the Byzantine Empire to soldier on until 1453.

The Great Migrations

After a period of tribal infighting, a number of nomadic tribes from the Asian Steppes started crossing the Carpathian mountains. In the sixth century, Slavs settled in Serbia, from where they expanded across much of the southern Balkans. The Avars arrived in Romania and Hungary in AD568, while the Bulgars captured Moesia from the Byzantines in AD681, creating the first Bulgarian kingdom. Apart from a brief return to Byzantine rule in 11th–12th centuries, the Bulgars remained in power until overrun by Ottoman Turks in 1396. The Magyars came to the region after AD830, at first trying to dislodge the Bulgars, but when this failed they turned north to take Romania and Hungary from the Avars in AD895.

Hungary and the Magyars

The Magyars, led by Árpád, settled Hungary between various tribal groups. The conversion to Catholic Christianity in 1000 of King Istvan I (Stephen I), who was canonised as Szent Istvan, and adoption of western European script and methods of government, established the country as a European nation. Over the next 500 years a succession of kings steadily expanded the Greater Hungarian Kingdom and by the beginning of the 16th century in addition to Hungary and Transylvania (northern Romania) it included all of modern day Slovakia, much of Croatia plus parts of Austria, Poland, Serbia and

Árpád, leader of the Magyars, is commemorated in Ráckeve (Stage 1)

Ukraine. However a peasants' revolt in 1514 and disputes between the king and his nobles left the country in a weak position between two other powerful empires, the Ottoman Turks and Austrian Habsburgs.

Ottoman Turks

Having captured Bulgaria in 1396 and the Byzantine capital Constantinople (modern day Istanbul) in 1453, the Islamic Ottoman Turks continued to move north. In 1525, as part of long held ambitions to extend their territories across the Balkans into central Europe, they formed an alliance with France aimed at confronting the power of the Habsburg-dominated Holy Roman Empire. After taking

The battlefield at Mohács where defeat by the Ottoman Turks ended the Hungarian Kingdom (Stage 6)

Belgrade (1521), then a Hungarian city, the Turks were well placed to march upon the Habsburg capital, Vienna. To do so they first had to conquer Hungary. In 1526 the advancing Turks routed a Hungarian army, commanded by King Ladislaus II, at the Battle of Mohács (Stage 5), and although the King managed to escape he drowned crossing the river. Many Serbs and Hungarians fled before the arrival of the Ottomans who captured Budapest unopposed and went on to lay siege to Vienna in 1529, although they failed to capture it. The death of King Ladislaus, who had no heir, marked the end of the independent Hungarian Kingdom, the crown passing by marriage to the Austrian Habsburgs, who ruled what was left of the country from Pressburg (modern day Bratislava). Southern Serbia was annexed by the Ottomans in 1540.

For nearly 160 years the Turks controlled the lower Danube basins, ruling over a mainly empty land, the Christian population having either fled or been slaughtered. A number of attempts to push further into western Europe were unsuccessful, culminating in defeat at the second siege of Vienna (1683), a battle that was hailed by the Catholic Church as the deciding victory of Christianity over Islam in Europe. The Turks were gradually pushed back through Hungary by Habsburg forces, before being expelled from Hungarian territory after the Battle of Belgrade (1688). They did however retain control of southern Serbia, Wallachia (southern Romania), Dobruja (Danube Delta) and Bulgaria.

The Habsburgs

The House of Habsburg, which origi-
nated in 11th-century Switzerland,
came to prominence when Rudolf
von Habsburg became king of
Germany (1273) and Duke of Austria
(1282). After becoming the dominant
force in the Holy Roman Empire, a
series of dynastic marriages expanded
Habsburg power over Spain and its
American colonies, Burgundy, the
Netherlands, Bohemia and much of
Italy. Along the Danube they controlled Austria itself, the Austrian
Vorland (modern Württemberg) and
Slovakia after 1526. When Prince
Eugene of Savoy, commanding
Habsburg forces, drove the Turks out
of Hungary in 1687, Hungary and
its territories in Croatia, Vojvodina
(northern Serbia) and Transylvania
(northern Romania) all came under
Habsburg rule. The Habsburgs repop-
ulated the empty lands with returning
Hungarians and Serbs plus large numbers of Swabian Germans who had
been displaced from Germany by the
Thirty Years War. The Danube was the
major transport corridor linking this
empire together.

Independence movements

In 1848 the Austrians put down a violent uprising, seeking Hungarian independence. However, the Hungarians
did gain a measure of self-government
under the overall rule of the emperor,
with the Habsburg possessions being
rechristened in 1867 as the Austro-
Hungarian Empire. At the same time

there were unsuccessful uprisings by
the Serbs in Novi Sad against their
Austrian rulers and by Romanians
in Wallachia against Ottoman rule.
Although these were put down by a
combination of Russian and Turkish
forces, they started a process by
which Wallachia and Moldavia
gained independence (as Romania)
from Turkey during the Russo-Turkish
war of 1877–1878. This same war
also saw Bulgaria and Serbia escape
from Turkish rule and represented
the beginning of Russian interest and
influence in the region.

The First World War and its consequences

The shots that started the First
World War (1914–1918) occurred
in Sarajevo (Bosnia) when a Serb
nationalist assassinated the heir to
the Austro-Hungarian throne. Austria
retaliated by attacking Serbia, starting a snowball effect in which a series
of alliances drew almost all of the
nations of Europe into the conflict.

The Treaties of Versailles (with
Germany), St Germain (with Austria),
Trianon (with Hungary) and Sevres
(with Turkey), which followed the
war in 1919–1920, had an enormous
effect on both the Austro-Hungarian
and Ottoman Turkish empires. The
Habsburgs lost their throne after
over 600 years and their empire was
dismantled with Romania gaining
Transylvania and Slovakia becoming part of the new country of
Czechoslovakia. Hungary and Austria

From Zemun (foreground) the first shots of the First World War were fired at Belgrade (far distance) across the river Sava (Stage 11)

were left as two small independent nations. In Turkey, the Ottomans were removed and their empire dismantled. The new kingdom of Serbs, Croats and Slovenes, which included Serbia and territories once controlled by both Austro-Hungarians and Ottoman Turks, gained the most. In 1929 it assumed the name of Yugoslavia (literally 'land of the south Slavs'). There was an extensive movement of peoples, particularly of Hungarians leaving Transylvania and Vojvodina.

In Germany the effect was mostly economic, with large reparation payments and inflation leading to national bankruptcy and political unrest. The Nazi party, led by Adolf Hitler, took advantage of this upheaval, taking power in Germany in 1933 with a policy that included overturning Versailles and expanding German territory. A referendum in Austria (1938) led to the Anschluss, political union between Germany and Austria under Nazi control. German invasions of Czechoslovakia and Poland led to the Second World War (1939–1945), with Hungary, seeking to regain territory lost in Trianon, joining the German-Austrian Axis. For a variety of local reasons, Romania, Bulgaria and the Croatian part of Yugoslavia also supported the Axis powers. The Germans invaded Yugoslavia (1941), where they met fierce resistance from communist partisans led by Josip Tito. After the failure of Germany's attempt to invade Russia (1942), Russian forces slowly got the upper hand and pushed German forces and their allies back through central and south-eastern Europe.

Iron Curtain and communism

Defeat of the Axis powers in the Second World War led to the lower Danube coming under the control of the victorious Allied powers, specifically Soviet Russia. Bulgaria, Hungary and Romania were all forced to adopt communist systems of government with private property expropriated by the state and farms collectivised. Their economies and military capabilities were integrated with that of the Soviet Union under the terms of the Warsaw Pact. The economic and social consequences of this period are still very much in evidence, particularly in Romania. Large estates of poor quality social housing ring most towns and cities, while dilapidated ruins of Soviet era factories abound. The border between Soviet controlled eastern Europe and western Europe was heavily fortified by the Russians with a line of defences described by Winston Churchill as an Iron Curtain. An uprising against communism in Hungary (1956) was viciously put down by Russian troops.

Yugoslavia, now led by Tito, adopted a less rigid communist system and did so without coming under Russian control.

Yugoslav Civil War

Ever since its creation in 1919, Yugoslavia was always a disparate

The 1956 uprising against communism is commemorated by a monument in Budapest (Stage 1)

Vukovar war cemetery is the site of a mass grave of Croat victims of the Yugoslav Civil War, marked with 938 crosses (Stage 8)

country. Actions to create a unified nation, such as the adoption of a common language (Serbo-Croat) and integration of ethnic groups were only partially successful. Tensions between Muslim Bosnians, Catholic Croats and Orthodox Serbs were kept in check during the rule of Tito, but after his death in 1980, the country began to disintegrate. After Slovenia and Croatia seceded from the Yugoslav Federation in 1991, all out civil war started, with the Serb dominated Jugoslav National Army (JNA) being used in an attempt to stop the secession movement. Fighting was particularly intense along the Danube border between Croatia and Serbia, especially around Vukovar (Stage 7). Later the conflict spread to Bosnia and in all these regions military action was accompanied by atrocities against minority civilian populations. Leaders in all three countries have since been arraigned for war crimes.

Most fighting ceased in 1995, but a final twist to the war came in 1998–1999 when Serb forces tried to prevent Kosovo from seceding. This resulted in reprisal bombing of Serbia by NATO air power. Altogether it is estimated that 140,000 people died during the conflict, while a further four million were displaced as refugees, many permanently. Although the war is over, with former Yugoslavia broken-up into seven independent states, tensions still exist between Croat and Serb communities, with some damage still evident and unexploded ordinance remaining in conflict areas. However, there is no need to be worried as far as this journey is concerned. It follows a safe route through what was the front line between Serbia and Croatia.

17

European Union

Following the collapse of communism in 1989, Hungary, Romania and Bulgaria were quick in seeking new alliances within Europe. They all joined NATO and between 2004 and 2007 became members of the European Union. Croatia joined the EU in 2013 after difficulties had been settled arising out of the Yugoslav Civil War. Serbia, Moldova and Ukraine all have applications to join the EU pending. Hungary (2007) and Croatia (2023) have signed the Schengen agreement allowing barrier free trade and travel within the Schengen zone, while Romania and Bulgaria plan to do so. Only Croatia has joined the Eurozone monetary union, but euros are widely accepted and many hotel prices are quoted in the currency. Despite being a member of the EU, Hungary has a strong nationalistic movement that dreams unrealistically of returning the country to the pre-Trianon borders of Greater Hungary.

As history has shown, this is not the first time that the whole of the lower Danube region has been politically unified. The Romans, Ottoman Turks, German Nazis and Soviet Russians all forced unity upon the region. This time unity has been achieved by democratic means!

Shipping on the river

The Danube has been a major trade artery for centuries; indeed, Genoese sailors established a number of riverside settlements in Romania in

Cruise boats on their way to the Black Sea pass through the Iron Gates gorges (Stage 16)

medieval times. However, the existence of fast flowing narrows such as the Iron Gates gorges made navigation difficult and sometimes dangerous. Two huge dams have tamed this natural obstruction and large barges can sail all the way upstream to Germany where, by continuing on the Rhein–Main–Donau canal, they can reach the Rhine and eventually the North Sea. Tourist boats are a popular way of seeing the river. These mostly cruise between Passau and Budapest on the middle Danube, but some go all the way from Amsterdam to the Black Sea. Navigation on the river is controlled by an international commission. Distances on the river are marked by regular kilometre boards, which show the distance upstream from a 0km marker at Sulina near to the entrance to the Black Sea in the Danube Delta (Stage 32A).

THE DANUBE CYCLEWAY

The 1712km lower Danube Cycleway passes through four countries. The first 234km are in Hungary, followed by 540km through the former Yugoslav states of Croatia and Serbia. The remainder of the journey, 938km, is across the south of Romania, through the regions of Wallachia and Dobruja.

This route starts in the heart of Hungary's capital Budapest (Stage 1), before leaving the city via Csepel-sziget island and then following the Danube south across the Great Hungarian plain (Stages 2–5) to reach

the border with Croatia. After passing through Slavonia, a region of Croatia recovering from the Yugoslav Civil War (Stages 6–8), the Danube is crossed into the Serbian region of Vojvodina to visit the cities of Novi Sad and Belgrade (Stages 9–11).

Heading east through Serbia, using cycle tracks along long stretches of Danube flood dyke (Stages 12–14), the barrier formed by the Carpathian mountains is reached at Golubac. The next 150km is the most scenic part of the route as it follows the river through the deep and winding Iron Gates gorges traversing a gap between Carpathian (to the north) and Balkan mountains (to the south) (Stages 14–16). Emerging from the gorge before Drobeta-Turnu Severin, the route enters Romania and turns south following quiet country roads through a remote corner of Wallachia (Stages 17–18) to reach Calafat.

For over 430km from Calafat to Călăraşi (Stages 19–25) our route follows the Danube road (Strada Dunarii), a road built in the mid-19th century to link riverside towns and villages in newly independent Romania. By now the river is flowing through a wide valley with a flood plain up to 30km across bounded by a river terrace that typically rises 50m above the valley floor. The mostly level route passes through a seemingly endless series of villages along the side of this flood plain, climbing occasionally on and off the river terrace. A number of riverside towns are passed, all with

Veliki Kazan (Great Cauldron) is the narrowest part of the Iron Gates gorges (Stage 16)

declining populations and surrounded by the decaying hulks of abandoned Soviet era factories. The Danube road was once lined throughout by shade giving trees, but many of these have succumbed to disease and been cut-down.

At Călărași, where the Danube divides into two channels, the river is crossed and the going becomes hillier as the route undulates through the hills of southern Dobruja (Stages 26–27) following the eastern branch of the river. This undulating going continues as the route turns north through Dobruja, eventually reaching the foothills of the Măcin mountains (Stages 28–29). The final stages (30–32) circle these mountains, crossing

the river twice to visit the large cities of Brăila and Galați before ending at Tulcea, the gateway to the Danube Delta. An alternative stage (31A) after Galați allows you to pass through a small corner of Moldova and Ukraine while another (32A) extends the route from Tulcea by boat into the Danube Delta. There is an alternative route for Stages 27–32 through Dobruja, going from Ion Corvin to Tulcea via Constanța and the Black Sea coast.

On a trans-European level, the Danube Cycleway is part of EuroVelo route 6 which runs from St Nazaire on France's Atlantic coast to Constanța on the Black Sea and is the best developed of all EV routes. If you wish to cycle other parts of this route, the part

The Romanian Danube road was once tree-lined along its entire length (Stages 19–25)

6

Atlantic – Black Sea

from St Nazaire to Digoin in central France is covered by *The River Rhone Cycle Route* (ISBN 9781786310835), a section through the border area between France, Switzerland and Germany is in *The Rhine Cycle Route*

(ISBN 9781786311092) and the upper Danube from southern Germany to Budapest in *The Danube Cycleway Volume 1* (9781852847227); all by the same author and published by Cicerone.

NATURAL ENVIRONMENT

Physical geography

The course of the Danube below Budapest has been greatly influenced by geomorphic events approximately 30 million years ago, when the Alps, Carpathian and Balkan mountain ranges were pushed up by the collision of the African and European tectonic plates. The Carpathians rose in

Small farmers in Romania still make extensive use of horse-drawn carts

a large curved S-shaped formation, passing through what are nowadays Slovakia and Romania, while the Balkans continued this curve through Serbia and Bulgaria. The Danube has cut its way between these two mountain ranges by way of the Iron Gates gorges.

Either side of this mountain barrier, the river has created two extensive basins. The Pannonian basin takes up most of central Hungary (where it is known as the Great Hungarian plain) and extends south into Slavonia (eastern Croatia) and Vojvodina (northern Serbia). East of the mountains is the Wallachian basin, taking up the southern part of Romania. In both these basins the river has over many centuries changed its meandering course as a result of frequent flooding. This has created a swampy flood

plain close to the river. Bounding this flood plain and set back from the river sometimes by as much as 30km is the low rise (between 30–50m) of a river terrace leading to a fertile plateau of sandy loess (fine windblown soil) formed from silt brought down by the Danube. The construction of extensive flood dykes in the Pannonian basin and the Iron Gates dams, constructed in the late 20th century between the two basins, have permanently changed the pattern of regular flooding. This has enabled the flood plains to be developed agriculturally. Farming on the plateau above the river terrace is typically arable, with wheat, maize, oilseed rape and sunflowers the main crops cultivated in very large farms. On the floodplain, smaller farms grow a mixture of crops, fruit and vegetables in addition to

Mobile beehives on the back of large trucks are used to pollinate fields of rape and sunflowers in Romania

raising livestock. Traditional farming methods are followed in many areas, including local styles of haystacks in Serbia, mobile beehives pollinating the crops, extensive use of horse and carts in Romania and reed cultivation in the Danube Delta.

As the boundary between tectonic plates the region is subject to occasional earthquakes. Strong tremors greater than magnitude 7 occur on average every 58 years. The most recent (mag 7.4) was in 1986, while a mag 7.1 earthquake in 1977 severely damaged the Romanian town of Zimnicea (Stage 22).

Wildlife

While a number of small mammals and reptiles (including rabbits, hares, red squirrels, voles, water rats, weasels and snakes) may be seen scuttling across the track and deer glimpsed in forests, this is not a route inhabited by rare animals. European beaver, which had been hunted to extinction throughout the lower Danube during the 19th century, have been successfully reintroduced in a number of locations including the Gemenc national park (Hungary, Stage 4), Kopački rit nature reserve (Croatia, Stage 6) and river Olt (Romania, Stage 21) from where they have spread down river as far as the Danube Delta. As they are mainly nocturnal, your chances of seeing a beaver are slight, although you may spot a lodge. Wild boar are indigenous throughout the route, being particularly numerous in Kopački rit.

There is a wide range of interesting birdlife. White swans, geese and many varieties of ducks inhabit the river and its banks. Cruising above, raptors, particularly buzzards and kites, are frequently seen hunting small mammals. Birds that live by fishing include cormorants, noticeable when perched on rocks with their wings spread out to dry, and kingfishers. These exist in many locations, mostly on backwaters, perching where they can observe the water. Despite their bright blue and orange plumage they are very difficult to spot. Grey herons, on the other hand, are very visible and can often be seen standing in shallow water waiting to strike or stalking purposefully along the banks.

Perhaps the most noticeable birds are white storks. These huge birds, with a wingspan of two metres, nest mostly on man-made platforms. They feed on small mammals and reptiles,

which they catch in water meadows or on short grassland. They are common throughout the route, particularly in southern Romania where many villages have what looks like avenues of stork nests balanced precariously on almost every telegraph pole.

Among a wide variety of reptiles, dice snakes are common around Kopački rit while wild land tortoise can be found in Romania's Đerdap National Park (Stages 15–16).

When to go
The route is generally cycleable from April to October. The best times are probably late spring (May–June) and early autumn (September–October) as it can be very hot during July and August when 40°C is not uncommon on the Hungarian plain and in southern Romania.

How long will it take?
The main route has been broken into 32 stages averaging 53.5km per stage, although there is a wide variation in stage lengths from 30km (Stage 30) to 96km (Stage 19). A fit cyclist, cycling an average of 90km per day, could complete the route in 19 days. However, the main determinant of how long the trip will take is not the distance you can cycle in a day; rather it is the distance between accommodation options, particularly in Romania. Unless you are camping,

Most villages in southern Romania have a number of stork nests, like this one in Năvodari (Stage 22)

or are sufficiently fluent in Romanian to ask around in villages for private accommodation, you will find it difficult to achieve a steady daily distance and should allow at least three weeks for the journey. Travelling at a gentler pace of 60km per day and allowing time for sightseeing, cycling from Budapest to the Black Sea would take four weeks.

What kind of cycle is suitable?

Most of the route is on asphalt surfaced roads or cycle tracks. However, there are some long stretches of cycling along unsurfaced flood dykes in Hungary and Serbia, and some of the road surfaces in Romania leave a lot to be desired although since Romania joined the EU they are improving rapidly. As a result, cycling the route as described in this

guide is not recommended for narrow tyred racing cycles. There are on-road alternative routes which can be used to by-pass the rougher off-road sections. The most suitable type of cycle is either a touring cycle or a hybrid (a lightweight but strong cross between a touring cycle and a mountain bike with at least 21 gears). There is no advantage in using a mountain bike. Front suspension is beneficial as it absorbs much of the vibration. Straight handlebars, with bar-ends enabling you to vary your position regularly, are recommended. Make sure your cycle is serviced and lubricated before you start, particularly the brakes, gears and chain.

As important as the cycle is your choice of tyres. Slick road tyres are not suitable and knobbly mountain bike tyres not necessary. What you

A fully equipped cycle

need is something in-between with good tread and a slightly wider profile than you would use for everyday cycling at home. To reduce the chance of punctures, choose tyres with puncture resistant armouring, such as a Kevlar™ band.

GETTING THERE AND BACK

You may have reached Budapest by cycling the Danube Cycleway from Vienna or even from the river's source in the German Black Forest. If you did you will have reached Szechenyi chain bridge in central Budapest, the start point for Stage 1 of this guide. If you are starting from Budapest, you can reach the city by rail, air, road or river. Since covid restrictions greatly limited the carriage of bikes on Eurostar from London to Paris and Lyria TGV trains from Paris to Zurich

ceased carrying bicycles altogether, getting your bike from the UK to Budapest by train has become very difficult. The current best recommendation is to go by plane.

By air
Budapest airport receives direct flights from all over Europe. Airlines have different requirements regarding how cycles are presented and some, but not all, make a charge that you should pay when booking as it is usually greater at the airport. All require tyres partially deflated, handlebars turned and pedals removed (loosen pedals beforehand to make them easier to remove at the airport). Most will accept your cycle in a transparent polythene bike bag, although some (particularly EasyJet) insist on the use of a bike box. Cycling UK have designed a polythene bike bag

BUDAPEST AIRPORT TERMINAL 2 TO FERIHEGY STATION

To reach Ferihegy by cycle, leave T2 from lower (arrivals) level and turn R. Continue past end of airport buildings and follow covered path (sp parking). Pass extensive car parking area R then dogleg L and R over car park entrance road. Pass aircraft museum L and continue on cycle track parallel with road L. Follow cycle track crossing side road and bearing R (sp main gate) to reach gate J (gate J is permanently open, ignore old sign that states entry with permission only). Continue ahead through gate and turn L opposite fuel depot, still following cycle track, to reach roundabout. Follow cycle track turning R across road, then pass under motorway and continue on cycle track clockwise around second roundabout. Leave by fourth exit, passing McDonalds L, on cycle track parallel with motorway and follow this for 3km to reach Ferihegy station. From here regular trains with cycle provision run to Budapest Nyugati station.

which can be obtained from Wiggle (www.wiggle.co.uk). Cardboard bike boxes can be obtained from most cycle shops, usually for free. However, you do have the problem of getting your box to the airport. If flying through Heathrow, Gatwick or Luton, airport branches of Excess Baggage Company (www.excess-baggage.com) sell bike boxes for £35. They should be contacted in advance to ensure a box is available.

All flights to Budapest arrive at terminal 2, which is 6km from the now closed terminal 1 and adjoining airport rail station at Ferihegy, on the opposite side of the airport. The connecting bus service does not carry bikes, however there is a continuous cycle track around the airport perimeter linking terminal 2 and Ferihegy station.

By rail

International rail services allow passengers to reach Budapest from all over Europe.

If travelling by rail from the UK, you can take your cycle on Eurostar from London St Pancras (not Ebbsfleet nor Ashford) to Paris Gare du Nord.

Before March 2020, all Eurostar trains carried up to six cycles, two fully assembled plus four disassembled packed in special fibre-glass cases which Eurostar supplied. Unfortunately this service ceased during the covid pandemic. When service restarted in January 2023 it was restricted to only a few trains carrying disassembled bikes prepacked by the customer. The effect is to make taking a bike by Eurostar the same as taking it by plane where you pack your own bike and hand it over at the station/airport for transportation. It is not known when (or even if!) full cycle carriage will recommence. Cycling UK's website (www.cyclinguk.org/eurostar) posts regular updates and has the latest information. Any changes to Eurostar policy will also appear on the updates page for this guide on the Cicerone website (www.cicerone.co.uk/1189/updates).

As of summer 2023, up to four pre-packed cycles can be carried on trains from London St Pancras to Paris Gare du Nord departing between 0755–1531. Booking must be made in

GARE DU NORD TO GARE DE L'EST

After arrival in Paris it is a short ride from Gare du Nord to Gare de l'Est. Go-ahead opposite Gare du Nord's main exit along Bvd de Denain, a one-way street with contra-flow cycling permitted. At the end turn L (Bvd de Magenta) then fork L at second traffic lights (Rue du 8 Mai 1945) to reach Gare de l'Est (5min). Do not be tempted to use the route signposted for pedestrians. Although this is shorter, it involves a flight of stairs.

advance by e-mail to travelservices@ eurostar.com Cost is £45 (€50) for bookings over 48hrs in advance and £60 (€70) for travel within 48hrs. Cycling UK members get a £5 discount. You must have a pre-purchased passenger ticket and travel on the same train as your bike. Bicycles need to be delivered pre-packed to the EuroDespatch counter beside the coach drop-off point behind St Pancras station at least one hour before departure. On arrival in Paris, bicycles must be collected directly from the train.

Frequent high-speed TGV Est trains run from Paris Gare de l'Est to Strasbourg, some of which have reservable bicycle spaces. Details and bookings on SNCF (French Railways) website www.sncf-connect.com. Reservations (€10) are mandatory for cycles and must be purchased in advance with your passenger ticket.

In Strasbourg a local service connects across the Rhine with DB (German Railways) for connections across Germany to Munich from where two-hourly high-speed Railjet trains will take you and your cycle on to Vienna and Budapest. Booking for German trains is on www.bahn.com.

An alternative is to catch the overnight Nightjet train from Amsterdam to Vienna, which has reclining seats, couchettes and sleeping cars together with cycle provision. This can be reached by using DFDS ferries from Newcastle via Ijmuiden. Alternatively, Stena Line ferries from Harwich to Hoek van Holland or P&O ferries from Hull to Rotterdam with connections by train to Utrecht, will allow you to join the Nightjet at Utrecht, its first stop after Amsterdam. On Hoek van Holland ferries, through tickets allow you to travel from London (or any station in East Anglia) to any station in the Netherlands.

Up to date information on travelling by train with a bicycle can be found on a website dedicated to worldwide rail travel: 'The man in seat 61' www.seat61.com.

By road
If you travel by car you can leave it in Budapest and return by train via Bucharest when you have completed your ride. Budapest is between 1550km and 1600km from the Channel ports depending upon route.

By river
If you have the time and the money you can reach Budapest by using one of the many cruise boats that travel along the Danube. Most of these start from Passau on the German/Austrian border, but there are some that sail all the way from Amsterdam via the Rhine and the Rhein–Main–Donau canal.

Intermediate access
The only international airports passed are Osijek (Stages 6/7) and Belgrade (Stages 11/12). Giurgiu (Stages 23/24) or Oltenița (Stages 24/25) have the nearest railway stations to Bucharest airport.

While there are no railway lines that follow the river closely, many towns passed in Hungary, Croatia and western Serbia have stations, although in eastern Serbia and Romania stations are few and far between. Railway stations are listed in the text and shown on the maps.

Getting home
The best option is to take a train to Bucharest and fly home from there. Bucharest Otopeni (Henri Coandă) airport is 16km north of the city centre. Direct trains to the airport from Bucharest Gara Nord station run every 40mins with a 20min journey time. Flights operate from Bucharest to many international destinations. There are no bike boxes available at the airport, but there is a wrapping service that will wrap your cycle for a fee. Alternatively, Tulcea airport, 17km south of the city following Dn22, has daily flights to Bucharest while Constanța airport has domestic services to Bucharest and international flights to Istanbul.

You can return home by rail, although it is a long way by train from the Black Sea back to the cities of western Europe and even further to the UK. During high season (mid-June to mid-September) there is a daily direct train from Tulcea to Bucharest (which takes 5hrs 30mins) and all year there are two trains between Tulcea and Medgidia with connections to both Bucharest and Constanța. There are regular trains between Constanța

and Bucharest, but only a few of these officially carry cycles. Romanian train details can be found at www. cfrcalatori.ro. International trains link Bucharest Nord with Budapest Keleti and there is an overnight through train to Vienna. After Budapest you will need to retrace your outbound journey.

Waymarking
The Danube Cycleway has been adopted by the ECF (European Cyclists' Federation) as part of EuroVelo route EV6. Comprehensive waymarks incorporating EV6 have been erected through Hungary, Croatia and Serbia, but are not widely used in Romania.

In Hungary EV6 is well signposted, although two kinds of EV6 waymarks are used. Those with a green background indicate the final route while those on a yellow background represent a planned route that is not yet finalised. They appear in about equal numbers, but the number of green ('definitive') signs is increasing. In practise this system leads to some confusion, particularly where new green signs have been installed for a definitive route but not all yellow ones removed. If you follow the route described in this guide, about half the time you will be following green waymarks and the other half you will be following yellow ones.

Principal waymarks encountered: clockwise from top left, EV6 in Hungary (definitive in green, provisional in yellow), EV6 in Croatia, EV6 fingerposts in Serbia

Croatian EV6 Ruta Dunav waymarks originally appeared in the middle of long straight stretches of road and were of limited use for navigation. However the system has been extended to cover most junctions and is now fairly comprehensive.

Between 2007 and 2009 Serbia installed what was probably the most comprehensive waymarking system in Europe. EV6 Dunavska ruta finger posts were placed at every junction indicating three different kinds of route. Those with a red band show the definitive route, those with a green band an alternative asphalt route avoiding unsurfaced tracks and those with a purple band indicate side excursions to places of interest. Each sign carries a number which appears on the

definitive maps published by Huber Kartographie (see below) and a short aphorism in English, often a travel related quote from a leading writer or philosopher. Unfortunately many of these signs have not weathered well. Paint has blistered and faded, posts have become twisted to point in the wrong direction and some have disappeared altogether. It is still a good system, but without regular maintenance it is likely to deteriorate further.

In Romania there is no waymarking. However, as most of the cycleway follows one long country route, the Danube road, this is not much of a problem. Regular well maintained kilometre stones mark every road and can be useful in confirming that you are on the right route.

In the introduction to each stage an indication is given of the predominant waymarks followed.

Summary of cycle routes followed		
EuroVelo Route 6 (EV6)	Stages 1–16	Hungary/Croatia/Serbia
Ruta Dunav	Stages 6–8	Croatia
Dunavska ruta	Stages 9–16	Serbia

Maps

By far the best mapping is provided by the definitive maps of EV6 published by Huber Kartographie. These are available as an eight strip map set at 1:100,000 (ISBN 978 3 49375 296 0). Information is in German, but the mapping is clear and easy to understand. These maps are available from leading bookshops including Stanfords, London and The Map Shop, Upton upon Severn. Do not expect to find maps available en-route.

Various online maps are available to download, at a scale of your choice. Particularly useful is Open Street Map (www.openstreetmap. org) which has a cycle route option showing EV6. The ECF website has a downloadable map of the entire EV6, including the stages in this guide (www.en.eurovelo.com/ev6).

Hotels, inns, guest houses and bed & breakfast

Unlike the upper and middle Danube, where accommodation is plentiful, for most of this route places to sleep are more limited with sometimes long distances between them. This becomes more acute the further east you progress. Until recently it was impossible to complete this route without using a tent to provide accommodation in remote areas. However, the number of places offering accommodation has increased as new premises have opened and it is now possible by using Google search and websites such as www.booking.com to find accommodation all along the route. The stage descriptions also identify all places known to have accommodation.

Hotels vary from a few expensive five star properties to more numerous local establishments. Hotels and inns usually offer a full meal service; guest houses do sometimes. Signs showing in Hungarian *szoba*, Croatian *sobe*, Romanian *cazare* indicate that accommodation is available. In Hungary best value is often found in a *panzió* (pension) or *vendégház* (guest house). Prices for accommodation in all countries are significantly lower than in western Europe.

Most of the cities and towns passed through in Hungary, Croatia and Serbia have tourist offices with

*Dunavski Plićak cyclists' guest house beside the Danube
flood dyke in Manastirska Rampa (Stage 13)*

websites listing all accommodation in both the urban area and surrounding villages. These are listed in Appendix B. In Serbia, the national tourist office (TOS) has a website www.srbija.travel/en/accomodation that lists accommodation by cities and towns drawn from local tourist information offices.

Until recently there were no local tourist offices in Romania. However a national organisation, the Centrul Naţional de Informare şi Promovare Turistică (CNIPT) has been set up with the objective of opening local tourist offices in major towns and cities. Those on the cycle route are listed in Appendix B, although their numbers are growing as more

are being opened. They are readily identifiable as most are housed in small circular pavilions. In addition, Romania Tourism (roma-niatourism.com), a not-for-profit tourist organisation working closely with CNIPT, has a website listing accommodation, but this only covers major cities and popular tourist regions. Where there are long distances between places to stay, it is advisable to telephone ahead to ensure accommodation is available. It is sometimes possible to find accommodation by asking around in villages, but as few Romanian villagers speak any foreign languages, this is far from easy.

Youth hostels

Apart from four associated hostels in Budapest and four in Belgrade, there are only two Hostelling International youth hostels on the route, at Osijek in Croatia (Stage 6) and Novi Sad in Serbia (Stage 9). There are, however, independent hostels in major towns and cities that cater for backpackers. Many of these can be found via either www.hostelworld.com or www.hostelbookers.com.

Camping

If you are prepared to carry camping equipment, this may appear the solution to the problem of finding accommodation, particularly in Romania. However, official campsites, which are shown in the text, are few and far between. Camping may be possible in other locations with the permission of local landowners. The Romanian countryside is a surprisingly populous place, with many stages passing through a never ending string of villages, which often makes it difficult to find a spot to camp where you will not be observed or disturbed. Where there are campsites, these often have basic cabins to rent in addition to places to pitch tents.

Basic cabins can often be found at Romanian campsites such as these at Zăval (Stage 19)

33

FOOD AND DRINK

Where to eat

Compared to the upper Danube, the number of places where cyclists can find meals and refreshments is quite limited, particularly in Romania. Locations of all places known to have restaurants, cafés or bars serving food are listed in the stage descriptions. A restaurant is an *étterem* (Hungarian), *restoran* [ресторан] (Croatian/Serbian). Menus in English or German are sometimes available in big cities and tourist areas, but are rare in smaller towns and rural locations. Indeed, in smaller establishments there may be no written menu and even when a menu is provided only a few of the items listed will actually be available (the normal custom is for prices to be shown only for available items). In Romania every village has a number of small grocery stores that sell soft drinks, water and beer to consume on the premises, but meals and snacks are not available. There is, however, no problem purchasing bread, cheese, cold meats and salad items to put together a picnic lunch. Bars seldom serve food.

Paprika, an essential ingredient in Hungarian cuisine, on sale in Budapest's central market

When to eat

Breakfast (Hungarian *reggeli*, Croatian *doručak*, Romanian *mic dejun*) is usually continental: breads, jam and a hot drink. In Romania this is often supplemented with eggs, cold meats, cheese and fresh vegetables.

Lunch (Hungarian *ebéd*, Croatian *ručak*, Romanian *prânz*) is usually the main meal of the day. For a cyclist this can prove problematic, as a large lunch is unlikely to prove suitable if you plan an afternoon in the saddle. This is particularly pronounced in Romania where lunchtime menus often have no light meals or snack items, apart from soup.

For dinner (Hungarian *vacsora*, Croatian *večera*, Romanian *cina*) a wide variety of cuisine can often be found, both national and international. Pork and chicken are the most common meats and beef steaks, pasta and pizza are widely available. There are, however, national and regional dishes you may wish to try.

What to eat

Hungarian cuisine is most well-known for dishes that use ample quantities of paprika (mild red pepper). Goulash (boiled beef and vegetables, flavoured with paprika) is the national dish and appears on most menus as both a soup (*gulyásleves*) and a main course stew (*székelgulyás*). Paprika is also a key ingredient in chicken paprikásh (*csirkepaprikás*), a casserole of chicken and vegetables thickened with sour cream. Roast goose

is a favourite dish for celebrations. Stuffed cabbage (*töltött káposzta*) and stuffed peppers (*töltött paprika*) are both borrowed from Ottoman cuisine. Pancakes (*palascinta*) can be either savoury (such as *hortobágyi palacsinta*, filled with veal stew) or sweet, with jam, chocolate sauce or cream cheese. Other desserts include *somlói galuska*, pieces of sponge cake soaked in alcohol and served with chocolate sauce and cream.

Croatian and Serbian cuisine are very similar, both being influenced strongly by Middle Eastern ways of cooking assimilated during many years of Turkish occupation. *Čevapi* or *čevapčići* (spiced meatballs), *pljeskavica* (minced meat patties similar to a hamburger) and *ražnjiči* (kebabs), all often served with green peppers and *ajvar* (tomato, pepper and aubergine sauce), are widely found in snack bars and restaurants. Other meats include pork, lamb, veal and beef. *Karađorđeva šnicla* (Karadjordje's steak), rolled stuffed veal or pork, breaded and baked, is also known as maiden's dream because of its erotic shape. Many small restaurants along the Danube may only serve fish, mostly *šaran* (carp), *som* (catfish), *štuka* (pike) or *pastrva* (trout). Commonly found snacks include different kinds of *burek*, greasy filo pastry pasties filled with cheese, meat or spinach.

Romanian meals usually start with *ciorbă* ('sour' soup) made with either *burtă* (tripe), *peste* (fish), *văcuță* (beef) or *legume* (vegetables). A popular main course is *tochitură* (hearty meat stew in a spicy red pepper sauce) served with *mămăligă* (maize-meal polenta), cheese and a fried egg. *Mici* are small flat grilled minced pork patties, often sold by number from street vendors, while *sarmale* are cabbage leaves stuffed with meat and rice. Near the Danube, and throughout the delta, fish is abundant, most commonly *crap* (carp), *somn* (catfish) and *ştiucă* (pike). The most common dessert (in smaller restaurants often the only dessert) are *clatite* (pancakes) served with chocolate or jam.

What to drink

Hungary, Croatia, Serbia and Romania are all both beer and wine drinking countries. Beer is mostly lager style, and although apparently produced by a number of national breweries, large multinational brewers own most producers. Draught beer (Hungarian *csapolt sör*, Croatian *točeno pivo*, Romanian *bere la halba*) is widely available. In all four countries wine (Hungarian *bor*, Croatian *vino*, Romanian *vin*) quality suffered from a pursuit of quantity during the communist era, but has been steadily recovering since.

In Hungary vineyards spread throughout the country produce large quantities of table wine, mostly from kadarka red grapes or olasz white grapes (a variety of riesling). More well-known are full-bodied golden white wines, slightly sweet but fiery and peppery and an ideal accompaniment to spicy Hungarian food, and Bull's Blood, a full-bodied red made from bikavér grapes. Most famous of all is *tokay*, a dessert wine from north-east Hungary made by a unique process where the sweet pulp of over-ripe rotted furmint grapes (known as *aszú*) is added to barrels of one-year-old wine and left to mature for at least three more years.

In the former Yugoslav countries the tendency is for white wine to be produced inland to the north in Slovenia, northern Croatia and Vojvodina (northern Serbia) while red wine comes mostly from the south and the coastal regions of eastern Croatia, southern Serbia and Macedonia. The Danube valley is a major white wine producing area in both Croatia and Serbia, with Croatian vineyards on the slopes of the Bansko Brdo ridge (Stage 6) and around Vukovar and Ilok (Stages 7 and 8). This wine region extends into the Serbian foothills of the Fruška Gora mountains (Stage 10), with further Serbian vineyards south of Belgrade. Principal varieties are graševina (a local grape), traminer and Italian riesling. The main local red grape is prokupac, but this is declining in favour of international grapes such as cabernet sauvignon and merlot.

Romania is the world's ninth largest wine producer, but little is exported. Prior to the Second World War most of Romania's wine came from eastern Moldavia, an area that was annexed by the Soviet Union in 1945. The communist government replaced this lost acreage by planting state-operated vineyards, mainly in northern Wallachia, south of the Carpathians, which produced large quantities of cheap wine. Since the fall of communism many of these vineyards have been replanted with international varieties such as cabernet sauvignon, merlot, pinot noir, riesling and sauvignon blanc to produce better quality wine. Some local grapes have survived, the most common being fetească neagră (used for *roşu* (red) wine), fetească albă and fetească regală which both produce *alb* (white) wine. Tămâioasă grapes (similar to muscat) produce sweet wine. *Cotnari* is a sweet dessert wine very like Hungarian tokay, made from grasă grapes. The Danube passes close to two of Romania's better quality wine growing areas: around Segarcea (30km north of Cârna, Stage 19) and in southern Dobruja near Lipniţa (Stage 26) and around Murfatlar (Stage 27). One problem with buying wine in Romanian bars and restaurants is that it is almost always sold by the bottle (750ml) or by litre carafe. It is impossible to buy wine by the glass.

In all four countries the most popular spirit is fruit brandy. Hungarian *pálinka* can be distilled from apricots, plums or pears, while Croatian and Serbian *šljivovica* (sometimes called *rakija*) and Romanian *ţuică* are plum brandies. All are frequently home distilled, particularly in Romania and can vary from smooth and sweet to strong and fiery.

All the usual soft drinks (colas, lemonade, fruit juices, mineral waters) are widely available. Tap water is normally safe to drink in all four countries although if you are susceptible to stomach upsets caused by water that differs from your domestic supply, bottled water is on sale everywhere.

AMENITIES AND SERVICES

Grocery shops
In Hungary, Croatia and Serbia all cities and towns passed through have grocery stores, often supermarkets, and most have pharmacies. In Romania every village has a number of small general grocery stores often with a table and chairs outside where local residents can be found drinking beer at any time of day.

Cycle shops
Cycle shops and repair facilities are few and far between, particularly in Romania. A basic knowledge of cycle maintenance, particularly mending a puncture, adjustment of brakes and gears, replacement of broken spokes and repairing a broken chain might come in useful.

Currency and banks
The Hungarian currency is the Forint, although many tourist oriented businesses such as hotels and restaurants

Every Romanian village has a number of small grocery shops combined with a bar like this one in Ciocăneşti (Stage 25)

will accept payment in euros. Croatia switched from Kunas to euros in 2023.

Serbians use the Dinar, a direct successor of the Yugoslav Dinar while the currency in Romania is the Lei. In both countries the best rates of exchange are usually obtained by taking euros and exchanging them locally in registered exchange offices rather than banks; the days of an active black market are long gone. In both countries euros are widely accepted in tourist oriented businesses; hotel prices are often quoted in euros. Cross-exchange of local currencies is surprisingly difficult, even at border crossings. Because of this you should avoid changing too much currency as you may not be able to exchange it back after you leave the country.

Almost every town has a bank and many have ATM machines that enable you to make transactions in English. Contact your bank to activate your bank card for use in Europe.

Telephone and internet

The whole route has mobile phone coverage. Contact your network provider to ensure your phone is enabled for foreign use with the optimum price package. International dialling codes from the UK (+44) are:

- Hungary +36
- Croatia +385
- Serbia +381
- Romania +40

Almost all hotels, guest houses and hostels make internet access available to guests, usually free.

Electricity

Voltage is 220v, 50HzAC. Plugs are standard European two-pin round.

WHAT TO TAKE

Clothing and personal items

Even though the route is generally level, weight should be kept to a minimum. You will need clothes for cycling (shoes, socks, shorts/trousers, shirt, fleece, waterproofs) and clothes for evenings and days off. The best maxim is two of each, 'one to wear, one to wash'. The time of year will make a difference as you need more and warmer clothing in April/May and September/October. All of this clothing should be able to be washed enroute, and a small tube or bottle of travel wash is useful. A sun hat and sunglasses are essential, while gloves and a woolly hat are advisable in spring and autumn.

In addition to your usual toiletries you will need sun cream and lip salve. You should take a simple first-aid kit. If staying in hostels you will need a towel and torch (your cycle light should suffice). Mosquitoes can be a problem in rural areas in summer, particularly if camping, and both insect repellent and sting relief lotion should be carried.

Cycle equipment

Everything you take needs to be carried on your cycle. If overnighting in accommodation, a pair of rear panniers should be sufficient to carry all your clothing and equipment, but if camping you may also need front panniers. Panniers should be 100 per cent watertight. If in doubt, pack everything inside a strong polythene-lining

bag. Rubble bags, obtainable from builders' merchants, are ideal for this purpose. A bar bag is a useful way of carrying items you need to access quickly such as maps, sunglasses, camera, spare tubes, puncture-kit and tools. A transparent map case attached to the top of your bar bag is an ideal way of displaying maps and guidebook.

Your cycle should be fitted with mudguards and bell, and be capable of carrying water bottles and pump. Lights are essential for the many tunnels you will encounter passing through the Iron Gates gorges (Stage 15). Many cyclists fit an odometer to measure distances. A basic tool-kit should consist of puncture repair kit, spanners, Allen keys, adjustable spanner, screwdriver, spoke key and chain repair tool. It is prudent to carry basic spares including two spare tubes (essential), spare spokes and a chain link. On a long cycle ride, sometimes on dusty tracks, your chain will need regular lubrication and you should carry a can of spray-lube. A good strong lock is essential.

Customs requirements

Hungary, Croatia, Romania and Bulgaria are all members of the EU and there are no restrictions on taking your bicycle and equipment across borders between EU states, although as these countries are not in the Eurozone there are limits on the amount of currency that can be carried. As Serbia is not an EU member, you may be asked to complete a customs declaration form when entering the country declaring all items of value (eg money, jewellery, cameras, watches, computers and bicycles) and be able to account for these when leaving. The same applies if you use Stage 31A to travel from Galați to Isaccea via Moldova and Ukraine.

SAFETY AND EMERGENCIES

Weather

The lower Danube runs through the continental climate zone, typified by hot dry summers interspersed with short periods of heavy rain and cold winters when snow can lie on the ground for prolonged periods. The Black Sea coastal region has a milder climate that is slightly cooler and drier in summer and less cold in winter.

Road safety

Throughout the route, cycling is on the right of the road. If you have never cycled before on the right you will quickly adapt, but roundabouts may prove challenging. You are most prone to mistakes when setting off each morning.

Some of the route, mainly in Hungary, is on dedicated cycle paths; care is still necessary as these are sometimes shared with pedestrians. Use your bell, politely, when approaching pedestrians from behind. After Hungary most cycling is on country roads without a marked cycle lane, but as traffic is generally light this causes few problems. Indeed, in the whole crossing of Romania there are only three short stretches of cycle track. Road surface conditions are sometimes poor and a lookout needs to be kept for potholes. In Romania,

Average temperatures (max/min°C)							
	Apr	May	Jun	Jul	Aug	Sep	Oct
Budapest	16/8	22/12	25/15	27/17	27/17	22/13	15/8
Belgrade	18/8	23/13	26/16	29/18	29/18	24/14	18/9
Bucharest	18/6	23/11	27/14	29/16	29/15	25/11	18/6
Constanța	14/7	19/12	24/16	26/18	26/18	22/15	17/10

Average rainfall (mm/rainy days)							
	Apr	May	Jun	Jul	Aug	Sep	Oct
Budapest	42/6	62/8	63/8	45/7	49/6	40/5	39/5
Belgrade	56/13	58/13	101/13	63/10	58/9	55/10	50/10
Bucharest	46/7	70/6	77/6	64/7	58/6	42/5	32/5
Constanța	30/5	38/5	40/6	30/5	33/3	29/3	31/4

you will frequently encounter horse drawn vehicles. Be very careful at night as these seldom carry lights. Livestock can often be found grazing on the roadside, or even sitting on the road! Where cycling is on main roads there is often a wide cyclable hard shoulder.

Some city and town centres have pedestrian only zones. These restrictions are often only loosely enforced and you may find locals cycling within them; indeed, many zones have signs allowing cycling. One-way streets often have signs permitting contra-flow cycling.

None of the countries passed through require compulsory wearing of cycle helmets, but their use is recommended. Modern lightweight helmets with improved ventilation have made wearing them more comfortable.

Border crossings

In normal times, the borders between EU countries that have signed the Schengen agreement are open and border posts unmanned. Borders between non-Schengen EU members (in this guide Romania and Bulgaria) and between non-EU members

Danube cyclists passing the border with Bulgaria in Silistra (Stage 26)

(Serbia, Moldova and Ukraine) have border posts where passports must be shown. As the external boundary of the EU, some of these borders are a major point of arrival for immigrants and refugees seeking entry into Europe. At times of political tension border posts may be temporarily closed or have restrictions applied to control the flow of migrants. In such times, potential visitors should check before travelling to ascertain the prevailing position.

Emergencies

In the unlikely event of an accident, the standardised EU emergency phone number is 112. The entire route has mobile phone coverage.

Prior to January 2021, an EHIC card issued by your home country provided free access to medical care in state run establishments throughout the EU. When the UK left the EU, two changes occurred. Firstly a GHIC card replaced the EHIC card, although existing EHIC cards remain valid for up to five years until they expire. Secondly UK issued cards now only cover EU countries and neither GHIC nor EHIC cards are valid in Serbia, Moldova or Ukraine.

Theft

In general the route is safe and the risk of theft low. However, you should always lock your cycle and watch your belongings, especially in cities. The risk of petty theft is higher in Romania, particularly in areas with numbers of Roma children.

Dogs

In Romania semi-feral dogs roam freely in many villages, and can be a problem if they chase your cycle. However, if you stop and confront them, with your bike between you and them, they will normally back off. This problem is more pronounced in quieter areas, particularly between Hinova and Cetate (Stages 17–18) and Cernavodă and Măcin (Stages 28–29). You may wish to consider having an anti-rabies vaccination, although the risk of being bitten is low.

Insurance

Travel insurance policies usually cover you when cycle touring but they do not normally cover damage to, or theft of, your bicycle. If you have a household contents policy, this may cover cycle theft, but limits may be less than the real cost of your cycle. Cycling UK (formerly the Cyclists' Touring Club), www.cyclinguk.org.uk offers a policy tailored for your needs when cycle touring.

USING THIS GUIDE

Text and maps

There are 32 stages, each covered by separate maps drawn to a scale of 1:150,000.

Place names on the maps that are significant for route navigation are shown in **bold** in the route descriptions. Distances are measured to the centre of each town or village (usually the town hall or principal church) unless otherwise described and are cumulative within each stage. For each city/town/village passed an indication is given of facilities available (accommodation, refreshments, camping, tourist office, cycle shop, station) when the guide was written. This list is neither exhaustive nor does it guarantee that establishments are still in business. No attempt has been made to list all such facilities, as this would require another book the same size as this one. A facilities summary table can be found in Appendix A.

While the route descriptions were accurate at the time of writing, things do change. Temporary diversions may be necessary to circumnavigate improvement works and permanent diversions to incorporate new road developments. The Danube is prone to occasional flooding; exceptionally high floods in 2013 caused considerable damage, blockage to the route and diversions. In these instances you will usually find signs showing recommended diversions, although these may be in local languages only.

Some alternative routes exist and where these offer a reasonable variant, usually because of a better surface, they are mentioned in the text and shown in blue on the maps. There are a couple of opportunities to visit places of interest off the route. These excursions are described in the text and shown in purple on the maps.

Language

The English spelling of Danube is used throughout. In Hungarian the river is known as the Duna, in Croatian as the Dunav [Serbian; Дунае] and in Romanian as the Dunărea. An exception is made for compound proper nouns (Dunapart, Dunav–Tisa canal, Dunărea de Jos, etc). Place names and street names are given in appropriate local languages with the exceptions of Vienna (Wien), Belgrade (Beograd) and Bucharest (Bucureşti). See Appendix D for a language glossary.

During the Yugoslav period, Serbian and Croat, which have always been closely allied languages, were merged into one language, Serbo-Croat, with Latin spelling preferred over Cyrillic. Since the break up of Yugoslavia, nationalistic pressure in Serbia has presaged a move back to the use of Cyrillic lettering. In the Serbian stage descriptions, the Cyrillic spelling is given [in brackets] for all street and place names you may encounter on signposts. The Serbian Cyrillic alphabet can be found in Appendix E. Bulgarian and Ukrainian also use Cyrillic, although in a slightly different form.

STAGE 1
Budapest to Ráckeve

Start	Budapest, chain bridge (104m)
Finish	Ráckeve, Árpád bridge (100m)
Distance	47km
Waymarking	EV6

South of Budapest, the Danube divides into two arms, with the 48km-long Csepel-sziget island between them. After passing through the city's suburbs, the route follows the easterly Ráckevei-Duna arm before crossing onto the island and continuing to reach Ráckeve. This stage is completely flat.

BUDAPEST

In its heyday, Budapest (pop. 1,775,000) was an imperial city with splendour to match any in Europe. The catastrophe of the Second World War, followed by over 40 years of communism, left the city in a rundown state, with many of its elegant buildings dirty and crumbling. Much work has been done since 1989 to bring the city's architecture back to life, and the freshly cleaned honey coloured Süttő limestone of Budapest's principal buildings reflects a new optimism.

The current city is a result of an amalgamation (1872) between Buda, on a hillside west of the Danube, and Pest, on the flat floodplain to the east. Buda had developed as the royal city, first of Hungarian kings and later Habsburg Emperors. The hillside under the old castle district is riddled with a maze of defensive tunnels. During the Ottoman occupation, the Turkish governor ruled from Buda and fierce fighting during the liberation (1686) left the city in ruins. The houses, churches and buildings of the Royal Palace complex were built mostly in the 18th century on older foundations. The most famous landmarks in Buda are St Matthias church and the neighbouring Fishermen's Bastion, both in a highly eclectic 19th-century mix of Gothic, neoclassical and art noveau designs known as the Romantic style.

Buda is linked to Pest, the commercial and industrial heart of the city, by seven road bridges, all rebuilt after they were destroyed in 1944–1945. The oldest of these, Széchenyi Lánchid chain bridge (1849), built by British engineers, is a scaled up version of Marlow bridge over the Thames in England. Another British influenced building, the Hungarian parliament, which is the largest building in Hungary, dominates the riverfront. This was built when the Hungarian government returned to Budapest from Bratislava after 1848. The nearby neo-Gothic St István basilica was completed in 1905. A side chapel contains the hand of St István, the king responsible for introducing Christianity to Hungary. A number of grand boulevards were built in the 19th century. The most famous of these, Andrássy út, which connects Deák Ferenc tér square with Hősök tere (Heroes square), is lined with classical buildings including the Opera house.

The Ottoman occupation left its mark in the development of a number of bath houses. The most famous of these, Gellért baths in Buda and Széchenyi baths near Heroes square, were massively redeveloped during the 19th and early 20th centuries with impressive neo-Renaissance buildings. Another major influence came from a Jewish population that pre-Second World War had reached 250,000. The main synagogue, the largest in Europe, was severely damaged by Nazi supporters and many of its congregation died in concentration camps. Raoul Wallenberg, a Swedish diplomat, rescued others. The synagogue was restored in the 1990s and an Imre Varga sculpture of a weeping willow tree with the names of 400,000 Hungarian victims of the Holocaust inscribed on its leaves stands behind the main building.

Gellért baths

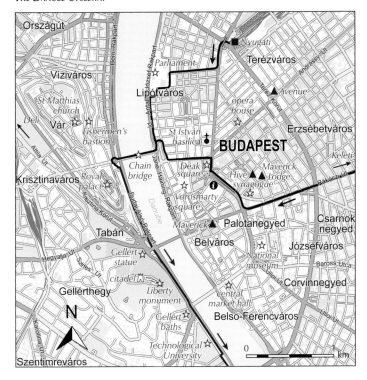

Getting to the start

Our route starts on the W side of **Széchenyi lánchid** chain bridge (104m). For those riders who have followed the Danube from its source, this is where your journey ended. If you are beginning in Budapest and have arrived at Budapest **Nyugati** station, it is a short ride on busy roads through the city centre. Bear R outside station front to reach a very busy intersection with traffic travelling in every direction. Turn L under flyover and follow Bajcsy-Zsilinszky út. Turn R at first traffic lights (Alkotmány utca) to reach Kossuth Lajos tér square in front of **Hungarian parliament**. Turn L and R to pass L side of parliament building then dogleg L and R following tram tracks into Széchenyi rakpart. Be careful not to continue onto the riverside boulevard. At Széchenyi Istvan tér, turn R onto chain bridge and cross river (2.5km from Nyugati).

From Budapest **Keleti** station, cross Baross tér in front of station and cycle west along main road (Rákóczi út) towards city centre. Continue ahead across first main boulevard (Erzsébet körút) to reach Astoria crossroads, with Astoria Hotel on corner L. Turn R (Károly körút) and pass Budapest **synagogue** on next corner R. At **Deák Ferenc tér**, where main road curves R, turn L across road and continue on other side with gardens of Erzsébet tér L. At end of gardens, turn L (József Attila utca).

Where this ends at Roosevelt tér, bear R into Széchenyi Istvan tér and follow road L around roundabout to reach chain bridge then bear R across Danube (4km from Keleti).

Once over bridge turn L at roundabout, where funicular climbs hillside ahead, then drop down L through gardens and across tram tracks to reach waymarked cycle route along riverside.

Budapest synagogue's willow tree memorial is inscribed with the names of Hungarian Jewish Holocaust victims

The route commences
Stage 1 begins by heading S away from chain bridge on cycle track beside Budai alsó rakpart riverside boulevard. Pass below **Royal palace** complex on hillside R and continue under Erzsébet hid bridge with **St Gellért statue** above R. Between this bridge and next bridge (Szbadság hid), wooded cliffside R is Gellérthegy hill, riddled with caves and water springs and crowned by fortified **citadel** and **Liberty monument**.

St Gellért, whose statue stands beside **Gellérthegy** hill, was an early Christian bishop who at the behest of King István, first Christian King of Hungary, attempted to convert the residents of Budapest to Christianity. He was murdered during a pagan uprising in 1046 by being pushed off the cliffs in a small cart. Atop the hill is a fortified Austrian citadel built after the Hungarian uprising (1848) to keep an eye on the citizens of the city below. Standing prominently on a white marble pillar in front of this bastion is the Liberty monument, a bronze statue of a lady holding a palm branch over her head. When erected in 1947, to commemorate the Soviet army's liberation of Budapest

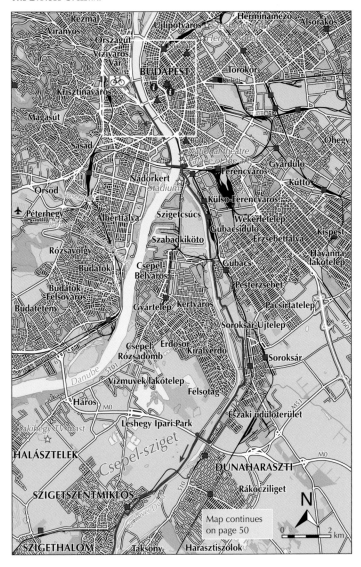

Map continues on page 50

N

0   2 km

from the Nazis in 1945, the lady was flanked by a Russian soldier carrying a Soviet flag. This element, and other Soviet embellishments, were removed in 1990 after the fall of communism and banished to a statue park on the edge of the city. Immediately below the hill is the Gellért thermal spa bath and hotel complex where you will find marble columned indoor and outdoor swimming pools, thermal baths, steam rooms, sauna and massage facilities.

Continue past Szbadság hid bridge with **Gellért Spa** hotel and baths R. Pass campus of **Technological University** and monument to victims of 1956 uprising both R. Where cycle track ends, dogleg R and L across main road to continue on opposite side of road in front of modern university buildings R. Pass under Petőfi hid bridge and continue alongside more modern university buildings. Just before next bridge (Rákóczi hid, recognisable by five red-rust coloured bridge towers), turn R away from river and follow cycle track beside slip road bearing L up onto bridge. Cross Danube (cycle track L), with **Budapest National theatre** visible L, then follow slip road bearing L down to other bank.

Just before roundabout, turn sharply L to follow Kornor Marcell Utca towards river passing modern **Palace of the arts** building R. Turn L under bridge (Hajóállomás utca). using cycle track L and continue past **National Athletics stadium** R to reach major crossroads. Go ahead over dual carriageway main road and after 80 metres, turn R, then R again on road across waste ground and immediately L through large stone gateposts into cobbled road passing derelict site L

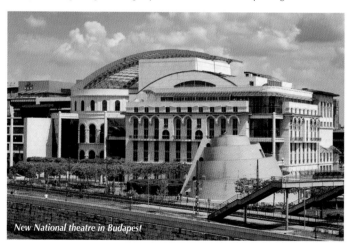

New National theatre in Budapest

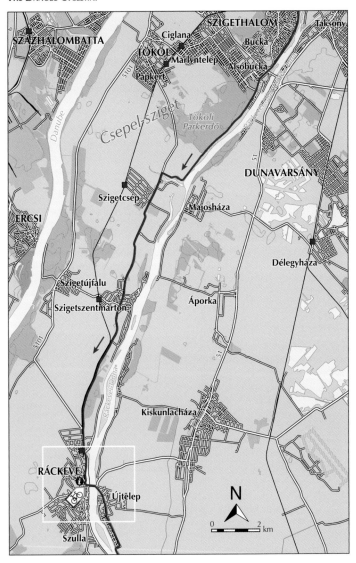

that once held the Budapest Trade Fair. Continue alongside Ráckevei-Duna arm of Danube, then bear R on gravel riverside track. R turn is easy to miss, it is just before start of long yellow wall on R. Pass under Gubacsi hid bridge and immediately turn L away from river. After 150 metres, turn R (Vizisport utca) into **Gubacs** (9.5km, 102m) (accommodation, refreshments, cycle shop, station).

Continue past Gubacs housing development L then straight ahead with rowing clubs on riverside R. Follow track bearing L and R, then turn R at T-junction past sewerage works L. Fork L on cycle track then turn R over small bridge and continue ahead through scrubland. After 1.5km, turn L at T-junction, then R at next junction. Bear L (Dobó utca) and turn R (Felsőduna sor) into **Soroksár** (13km, 100m) (accommodation, refreshments, station).

Cycle past houses and where road ends continue ahead on asphalt cycle track with backwater R. Emerge onto road and continue ahead. Where this turns L away from river, bear R ahead on cycle track. Turn R on small bridge over drainage ditch. Turn R in front of pink house to reach Ráckevei-Duna and L along riverbank road (Forster János Jakab utca). Where asphalt ends continue along Horgász part and on along Alsó-Duna sor. Just before motorway bridge on edge of **Dunaharaszti** (18km, 100m) (accommodation, refreshments, station), turn L and after 200 metres sharply R on cycle track beside motorway to cross river onto Csepel-sziget island.

Csepel-sziget is a 48km-long island between the main western arm of the Danube and the smaller eastern Ráckevei-Duna arm. It varies in width between 3km and 8km. While the northern end is mainly urban and makes up Budapest district XXI, further south the island is more rural with a series of commuter towns separated by agricultural land and areas of forest. A suburban railway runs down the island to Ráckeve.

Legend says it was originally settled by Árpád's tribe of Magyars, the island being named after Árpád's horse groom Csepel. Frequent floods and shifting water courses made the island difficult to cultivate and it became inhabited by successive waves of immigrants, first by Serbs in the 15th century fleeing the advancing Ottoman Turks and later by Germans in the 18th century invited in by the Hungarian state to settle the empty lands after the Turks were expelled. Remnants of both these colonisations remain. During the German period, the island was owned by Prince Eugene of Savoy who built a palace at Ráckeve. Major hydrological works in the early 20th century finally controlled the Danube. Sluices were built and flood dykes constructed to stabilise the two arms of the river and leave the Ráckevei-Duna arm as a navigable sidestream much valued for watersport activities and angling. The 314m transmission mast at Lakihegy is the tallest structure in Hungary.

Ráckeve sits beside the Ráckevei-Duna

Once over river, drop down and turn R back under bridge (Üdülő sor). Go ahead over railway level crossing into Rév út then turn L after house 2 (Liget utca), and first R (Biró Lajos utca) following one-way system. The L turn is easy to miss. At end, turn R on short stretch of dual carriageway (Május 1 sétány) then L (Horgász utca) past railway station in **Szigetszentmiklós** (23km, 96m) (accommodation, refreshments, camping, cycle shop, station).

Continue ahead for 3.5km parallel to river, which runs along behind houses L. Where road ends continue ahead for 300 metres on narrow riverside track then dogleg R and L to reach Mű út road junction (27km, 102m) (refreshments). The riverside track can be muddy when wet. Cross main road and go ahead on Dunasor utca. Bear L ahead at angled crossroads and pass series of café/bars (refreshments) R. Continue between woodlands of **Tököli** forest R and riverside houses L. The 650ha Tököli forest park is a popular green lung for Budapest with hiking trails and picnic places. Road becomes Parkerdő utca and continues past bus turning circle to reach road end at edge of forest (31.5km, 98m).

Bear L on 4wd track into scrubland and follow this bearing R to run parallel with river. Emerge at roadhead and continue ahead (Barátság utca) following this bearing R away from river. Turn L (Fő ut) at T-junction and cycle through **Szigetcsep** (34.5km, 100m) (camping, station). Continue through open country to reach **Szigetszentmarton** (39km, 100m) (accommodation, refreshments, camping, station). Pass through village on Kossuth Lajos utca and continue to reach beginning of Ráckeve. Pass entrance to Termálkristály spa hotel and Aqualand L then railway station and **Savoyai Kastély** hotel (both R), before following Eőtvős utca bearing R (part of town centre one-way system) to reach Árpád hid bridge in **Ráckeve** (47km, 100m) (accommodation, refreshments, camping, tourist office, cycle shop, station).

Ráckeve (pop. 10,600) is the main town of Csepel-sziget island. Despite legends attributing first settlement to the Árpád era conquest of Hungary by the Magyars (895–907), which is commemorated by a statue and Árpád museum, the town first came to prominence in the 15th century when Serbs from Kovin, fleeing from advancing Ottoman Turks, settled the area. Trading developed along the river and Ráckeve thrived with Serbian merchants building large houses on the riverside. The only Gothic style Serbian Orthodox church in Hungary dates from this period (1487). Later the Turks took Ráckeve too and remained for over 150 years. After their expulsion, when the Hungarian state invited German settlers to repopulate the reclaimed territory, Prince Eugene built (1702) the baroque Savoyai Kastély palace, in the town. The secessionist (art noveau) style town hall was built in 1901, at about the same time as the present day Árpád hid bridge replaced an earlier wooden structure.

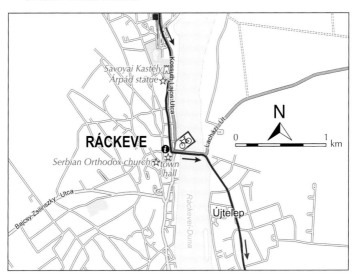

STAGE 2

Ráckeve to Solt

Start	Ráckeve, Árpád bridge (100m)
Finish	Solt, Béke tér square (97m)
Distance	50.5km
Waymarking	EV6

Continuing south, now on the eastern side of the river, our route follows mostly riverside roads and flood dykes across the Great Hungarian plain, passing through a number of villages and small towns. Some sections on flood dyke are unsurfaced and alternative routes are described to avoid these, though this may involve using a busy main road. There are few facilities in Solt, and an alternative stage end with more facilities can be reached by crossing the river to Dunaföldvár. The stage is completely flat.

The Ráckevei-Duna is a popular fishing river

From centre of Ráckeve, cross Árpád hid bridge over Ráckevei-Duna and turn R (Dömsödi út), passing spa and hotel L. Continue through town into area with houses R and open country L. Pass water tower and follow road bearing R by last house to reach Danube. Bear L (Kék-Duna sétány) along riverbank and continue for 6.5km, passing a continuous series of weekend riverside home developments to reach **Dömsöd** (9.5km, 99m) (accommodation, refreshments, camping).

After road moves away from riverside, turn R (Petőfi utca) at crossroads with basketball court R, then L (Középső Dunapart) to continue along riverbank. To reach the centre of Dömsöd, turn L at the crossroads and cross a bridge over the backwater. Where this ends, turn L over backwater bridge and R (Alsó Dunapart) to continue between river and weekend houses. After 7.5km, follow riverside road turning L away from river over drainage canal into **Szentgyörgypuszta** (18.5km, 95m) (accommodation, refreshments).

Zigzag R and L, then continue to reach T-junction. Turn R on road along flood dyke and cross drainage canal to reach second T-junction.

Between Szentgyörgypuszta and Dunaegyháza there are two stretches along unsurfaced flood dykes that can be difficult when wet. An alternative route avoids these, but does involve some cycling along a busy main road. The main and alternative routes come together in Dunavecse, then divide again.

Alternative route avoiding unsurfaced tracks

Turn L at T-junction then R at crossroads on edge of **Tass** (accommodation, refreshments) and follow route 51 (busy main road, no cycle lane) through **Szalkszentmárton** (28km, 94m) (accommodation, refreshments). Where route 51 bears L to by-pass Dunavecse, turn R towards village and immediately R again on gravel track. Follow this bearing L to reach flood dyke and turn L to temporarily rejoin main route.

Continue on asphalt track beside flood dyke, then climb onto dyke and fork R along top past **Dunavecse** L (33.5km, 98m) (accommodation, refreshments). Bear R onto road and just before end of village pass reconstruction of **ancient village** L. Continue to reach road junction just before motorway bridge. Here the route divides again.

Turn L on road beside motorway to reach roundabout. Turn R on cycle track R of main road (route 51) and continue under motorway bridge into open country. Where cycle track ends, turn R (Vasút utca, cycle track R) and follow this into **Apostag** (39km, 98m). Continue on road winding through village (Kossuth Lajos utca). Bear L (Bajcsy Zsilinszky utca) and continue out of village. Routes rejoin at end of Apostag.

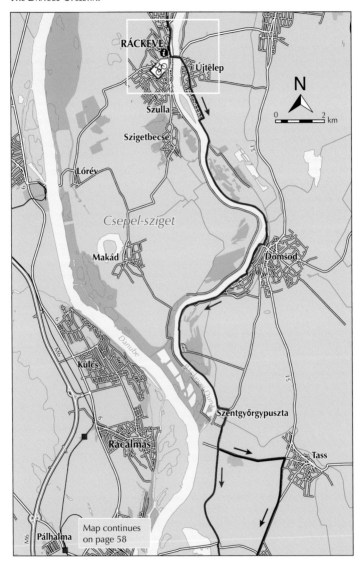

Map continues
on page 58

Main route along unsurfaced flood dyke

Continue ahead at T-junction through barrier along unsurfaced flood dyke for 11.5km, crossing a series of tracks with Dunaújváros steelworks visible on opposite side of Danube. Where dyke comes close to main road L, drop down R onto gravel track below flood dyke. The first section of alternative route rejoins here. Continue on asphalt track beside flood dyke, then climb onto dyke and fork R along top past **Dunavecse** L (33.5km, 98m) (accommodation, refreshments). Bear R onto road and just before end of village pass reconstruction of **ancient village** L. Continue to reach road junction just before motorway bridge. Here the routes divide again.

Go ahead on cycle track under motorway, which soon becomes unsurfaced track along flood dyke, and follow this for 3km. Pass Apostag behind fields L. Just after weekend home development turn L (Gátőr utca) to reach main road. Turn R, rejoining alternative route.

Combined route continues

Follow road through open country to **Dunaegyháza** (45km, 104m) (refreshments). Cycle through village on Országút utca and after 1.75km cross main road (route 52) and continue into **Petőfitelep** (47km, 99m) (accommodation, refreshments).

To visit Dunaföldvár

Turn R where road bears L into Petőfitelep on cycle track along dis-used railway track and cross Danube bridges into **Dunaföldvár** (accommodation, refreshments, camping, tourist office, cycle shop). Dunaföldvár is an attractive town with a wider choice of accommodation and food than in Solt.

The riverside spa town of **Dunaföldvár** (pop. 8400) has a restored rectangular tower from a 16th-century Turkish castle, which now houses a museum. The castle itself was destroyed in 1686 when the Turks withdrew. The nearby castle gateway is a highly decorated example of woodcarving by local artist Istvan Csepel. Further examples can be found in a woodcarving gallery in the castle grounds. The spa has indoor and outdoor pools with water at 36°C.

Main route continues to Solt

Follow road winding through **Petőfitelep**. After barely perceivable gap between villages, cycle track appears L and continues beside Posta utca. Pass **Vécsey palace** L and bear R to reach Béke tér square in centre of **Solt** (50.5km, 97m) (accommodation, refreshments).

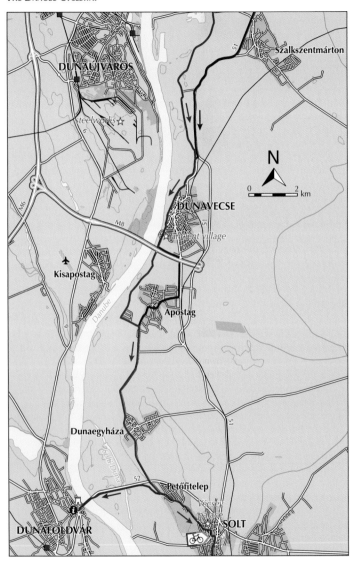

Dunaföldvár castle gateway

Solt (pop. 6900), a small town on the Great Hungarian plain with little to interest tourists, is named after Prince Solt, a son of Árpád and great grand-father of King István I, whose statue stands in the town centre. Vécsey pal-ace, a small neo-classical mansion, was built in 1816 for Count Vécsey, a general who fought against Napoleon and whose son, also a general, was executed by the Austrians during the 1848 Hungarian uprising. The mansion is now a library and its park contains a number of memorials including one to the 'martyrs of 1848'. The town's coat of arms features golden crossed keys, said to have been given to Solt in 1241 by King Bela IV in gratitude for being hidden in the town thus avoiding capture by invading Mongols. These were secreted at the top of the reformed church spire, but when this was hit by lightning, the keys melted and were never seen again.

STAGE 3
Solt to Foktő

Start	Solt, Béke tér square (97m)
Finish	Foktő (93m)
Distance	40.5km
Waymarking	EV6

Continuing along the completely flat east bank of the river, this stage follows flood dykes and quiet country roads through a succession of villages that form the heart of Hungary's main paprika growing region. The stage ends at Foktő, where there are limited places to eat and sleep. A short excursion will take you to Kalocsa with all amenities.

From Béke tér square in centre of **Solt**, head east (Törley Bálint utca) across small bridge over drainage canal to reach crossroads. Turn R on main road (Kossuth Lajos utca, route 51) passing church R and continuing out of town into open country. After passing sign showing 132km to Zombor, dogleg R and L onto cycle track along flood dyke parallel with main road.

Just after 96km marker, turn L across main road (sp Dunatetétlen), then after 600m turn R (sp Harta). Follow road through fields, then winding through **Harta** (13km, 94m) (accommodation, refreshments, camping) on Bajcsy-Zsilinszky utca to reach T-junction. Turn R, then immediately L, to second T-junction. Turn R (Kossuth Lajos utca) and follow this past church L to crossroads.

Go ahead over main road on quiet road towards Danube, soon joining cycle track L. At crossing of tracks, turn L beside sports ground R. Just before reaching forest (refreshments), turn L on track and follow this with fields L and riparian forest R. After 1.25km, turn sharply L at first following edge of forest, then turn R into forest to reach T-junction. Turn L and continue to reach cycle track along flood dyke beside route 51. Turn R, and continue parallel with road to beginning of Dunapataj. Cross main road and immediately bear L onto cycle track. This turn is easily missed. Follow this track curving round R to circle village. Continue ahead into Ujhelyi Imre utca and, where this bears R, continue ahead to reach crossroads. Turn R (Vásut utca) into centre of **Dunapataj** (21.5km, 94m) (accommodation, refreshments).

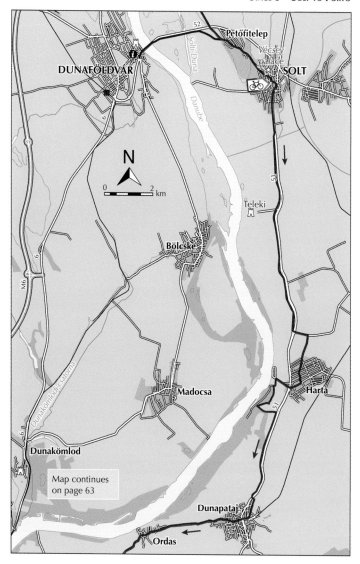

Map continues on page 63

Continue across roundabout into Ordasi utca (sp Uszód). Follow this out of village as it becomes a quiet country road through open country to reach **Ordas**. Beside the village cemetery is a hollow tree trunk holding a statue of Ferenc Rákóczi II (leader of 1703–1711 uprising against the Habsburgs) and his horse. Wind through village on Dózsa György utca then continue through open country to enter **Géderlak** (30km, 92m) on tree-lined Ordasi utca.

The statue of Ferenc Rákóczi II in Ordas is inside a hollow tree

Turn L in middle of village (Kossuth Lajos utca) and R by church (Dunaszentbenedeki út). After short stretch of open country, enter **Dunaszentbenedek** on Dózsa György utca. Turn L by church (Kossuth Lajos utca) and continue out of village using section of cycle track L. Where this ends continue along quiet road to reach **Uszód** (35.5km, 91m).

Go straight through village, on Szabadság utca, joining short stretch of cycle track R, and continue into open country. Turn L at roundabout with industrial area R and cross railway level crossing. Continue straight ahead over second roundabout (Josef Attila utca) to reach off-set crossroads in **Foktő** (40.5km, 93m) (refreshments).

To visit Kalocsa (4km off-route)

Turn L at off-set crossroads (Dózsa György utca). At village end this becomes a cycle track and continues beside road to reach first houses in Kalocsa. Turn L across road into Foktői utca and continue (using cycle path R) past military barracks L to reach Szentháromság tér in front of cathedral in centre of **Kalocsa** (4km from Foktő, 95m) (accommodation, refreshments, tourist office, cycle shop).

KALOCSA

Kalocsa (pop. 18,200) is one of the oldest towns in Hungary. After the conversion of the country to Christianity in 1000, it became the seat of an archbishop and second most important religious centre after Esztergom. By the 16th century the population had risen to 10,000. After the Turks conquered

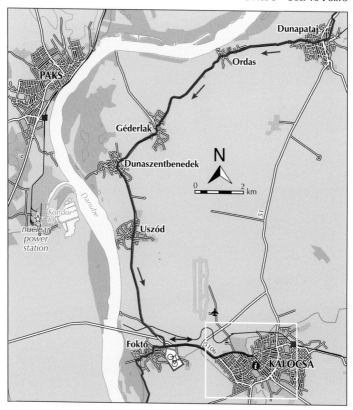

the city in 1543, most of the population fled and by 1580 there were only 350 inhabitants remaining. Turkish occupation ended in 1686 and the population recovered to over 5000 by 1700. Construction of a new cathedral commenced in 1735, the interior of which is sumptuously decorated in baroque style. The nearby archbishop's palace (1760) contains an ancient library with over 150,000 books. All the baroque buildings surrounding Szentháromság tér square are painted yellow in honour of Maria Theresa, Habsburg empress at the time they were built.

As a primarily religious centre, Kalocsa attracted little or no industrial development, the industrial estates around the town not being built until the 1960s. However, the town has a strong craft history, centred on design work featuring bright floral decoration for embroidery, ceramics and interior decoration.

Archbishop's palace in Kalocsa

The countryside surrounding Kalocsa is Hungary's main area for the cultivation of paprika peppers and in the autumn the fields are ablaze with red ripe fruit. Houses throughout town are festooned with strings of drying peppers and every September a paprika festival brings thousands of visitors, many in traditional floral costumes. A museum in Kalocsa is dedicated to the history, cultivation, processing and culinary uses of the spice.

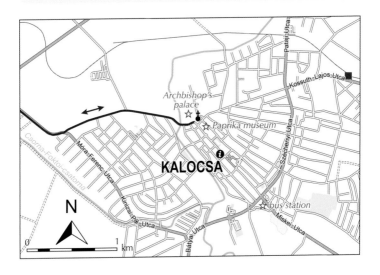

STAGE 4
Foktő to Baja

Start	Foktő (93m)
Finish	Baja, Szentháromság tér square (96m)
Distance	44.5km
Waymarking	EV6

Soon after leaving Foktő the route joins the Danube flood dyke, which is followed all the way to Baja. The whole stage is completely flat.

If you have visited Kalocsa, you first need to retrace your route to Foktő. Cycle W from off-set crossroads in **Foktő** (Fő út) and follow this turning second L. Cross small river bridge, then turn R opposite town hall (still Fő út). Pass church R and continue on Fő út winding through village. Fork R after house 123, then at end of village turn L onto 4wd track along Danube flood dyke and follow this to reach hamlet of **Meszesen** (5km, 91m) (refreshments, camping).

Go ahead over crossing of tracks, then fork L onto good quality gravel track along flood dyke. Follow this for 9km, with riparian woodland R and extensive views of Great Hungarian plain L, to reach crossroads with Dombori ferry road (14km, 91m). The red and white electricity pylon passed en route,

Paprika for sale by the roadside near Kalocsa

which takes cables across the Danube, is Hungary's tallest pylon at 138m. Here track becomes asphalt and continues ahead along flood dyke passing **Fajsz** L (refreshments) to reach motorway over-bridge (22.5km, 89m). Bear L under motorway and continue along flood dyke. The forested area on the opposite bank is Gemenc forest, part of Donau-Drava national park. After 11km, reach weekend

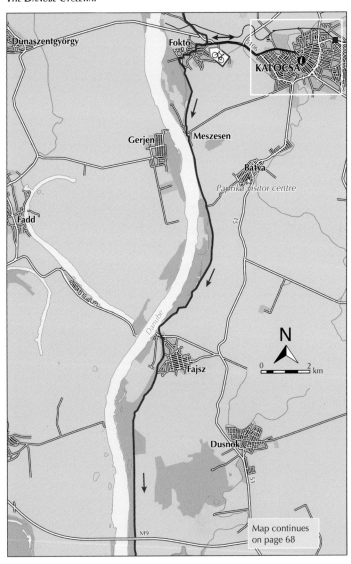

Dunaszentgyörgy

Foktő

KALOCSA

Gerjen

Meszesen

Bátya

Paprika visitor centre

Fadd

Danube

N

0 _____ 2 km

Fajsz

Dusnok

M9

Map continues
on page 68

home community of **Érsekcsanád** (34km, 89m) (refreshments) where there is a ferry across the river to the Gemenc national park visitor centre.

Stay on flood dyke and continue past a group of fishing lakes in old gravel quarry L. Pass sewerage works L, then eventually bear L past sluices. Turn R across small bridge over drainage canal to reach road junction. Go ahead under railway bridge (cycle track L), then just before railway level crossing turn R across road and L to join cycle track on opposite side. Cross railway and fork immediately R on cycle track along flood dyke. Follow this winding between factories and over two crossroads to reach river Sugovica. Continue ahead, now on Sugovica flood dyke, then emerge beside main road. Bear R, passing marina R, and continue behind riverside restaurants R to reach Szentháromság tér square in centre of **Baja** (44.5km, 96m) (accommodation, refreshments, camping, tourist office, cycle shop, station).

BAJA

Baja (pop. 35,000), on the banks of the Sugovica arm of the Danube, is a river port and local administrative centre. During the Turkish occupation it was a military and Islamic religious centre. After the Turks left, mostly Croats, Serbs and Germans repopulated the now empty town. In the 18th century Baja prospered from trading. Grain, wine and other agricultural products were shipped

Tóth Kálmán square in Baja

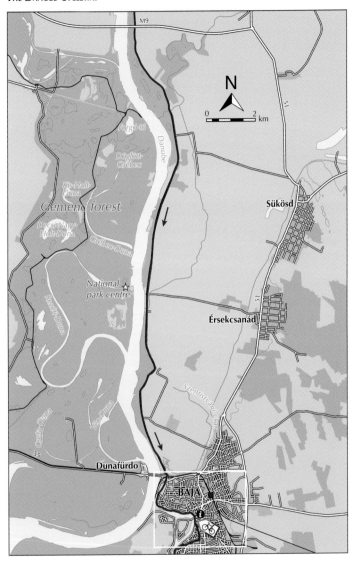

upriver to Austria and Germany, a prosperity that was enhanced by the coming of the railway in the 19th century and the growth of light industry in the 20th. Expulsions and resettlement after both world wars have resulted in the local population nowadays being 94 per cent Hungarian.

Renaissance style Szentháromság tér square, where you will find the Holy Trinity column and former Grassalkovich palace (now the town hall), faces the river. Pedestrianised Eôtvôs József utca links this square with Tóth Kálmán tér square and the parish church. In this square is a statue of Tóth Kálmán (1831–1881), local writer and poet, who after taking part in the 1848 uprising against Habsburg rule went on to edit a national newspaper and represent the town in the Hungarian parliament. Other notable buildings in Baja include the former synagogue, now the public library, and a Franciscan monastery plus churches for Catholic, Protestant and Orthodox communities. Petőfi island, across the Sugovica from Baja, is a recreational and sports area. Every July a festival is held where 2000 cooking pots of fish soup are cooked and served in the streets, justifying an entry in the *Guinness Book of Records*.

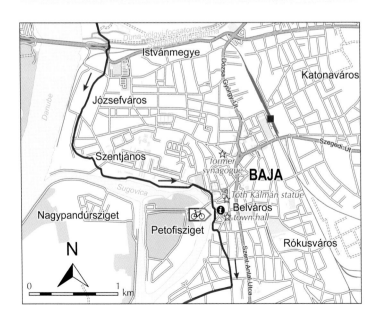

STAGE 5
Baja to Mohács

Start	Baja, Szentháromság tér square (96m)
Finish	Mohács, ferry ramp (86m)
Distance	34km
Waymarking	EV6

Apart from a short road section through the suburbs of Baja, this stage is entirely along the Danube flood dyke mostly past fields on the left and riparian woodland right. Again, it is completely flat.

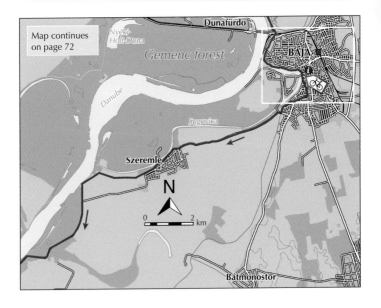

Map continues on page 72

The Votive church in Mohács was influenced by Islamic architecture

Leave Szentháromság tér square in **Baja** by south-west corner with Baja Wellness Hotel L. Turn L (Batthyány Lajos utca) and first R (Attila utca). Fork L (still Attila utca) and bear R onto main road (Szabadság utca). After 300m turn third R on concrete road (Hunyadi János utca). Pass Vöröskereszt tér, then where concrete surface ends, turn R (Kakas utca) on gravel track beside house 19. At end turn L into Szeremlei utca.

Pass harbour R and turn R at crossroads over bridge across canal. Bear L along road following flood dyke for 4.5km to reach beginning of **Szeremle** (7km, 87m).

Where road turns L into village, turn sharply R and after 50 metres bear L along flood dyke passing between Szeremle L and river Sugovica R. Continue along flood dyke beyond village, at first on good quality gravel track that becomes quiet asphalt road after 3.5km. This road eventually comes out alongside Danube and continues to reach **Dunafalva** (20km, 85m) (accommodation, refreshments, camping).

Pass ferry ramp and continue along flood dyke for 13km. Just after passing communications mast L, turn R at crossroads to reach ferry ramp in **Újmohács** (refreshments, camping). The ferry departs half-hourly at 10min and 40min past the hour; tickets must be bought from the kiosk marked 'Cassa' L of the café. Take ferry across Danube to **Mohács** (34km, 86m) (accommodation, refreshments, tourist office, cycle shop, station).

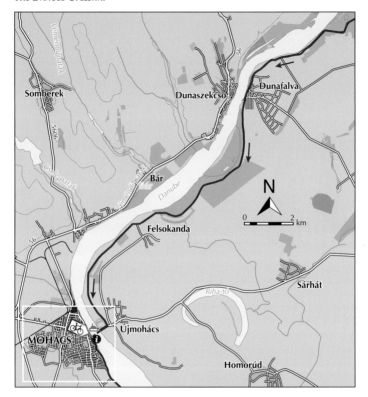

MOHÁCS

Mohács (pop. 19,000), the last town in Hungary, is best known as the location of the two battles of Mohács (1526 and 1687) that topped and tailed the Turkish occupation of the country. You will pass the 1526 battlefield on the next stage, but for now there is a museum in town with artefacts from the battle. The old Bishop's palace, now a boys' school, predates the occupation. Formerly the summer palace of the Bishop of Pecs, King Ladislaus II spent his last night here before the 1526 battle and his subsequent death. After falling to the Turks, Mohács became a government and administrative centre for the occupiers. Like many towns in Hungary, it was repopulated in the 18th century with an influx of Christian immigrants and still retains a multicultural atmosphere. Principal buildings include the town hall and Votive church, both of which include elements of oriental design, plus many churches serving the different national and denominational beliefs of the incomers.

Busójárás, the pre-Lenten carnival, attracts many visitors to Mohács. Participants, known as Busós, dress in sheepskins with cow horns on their heads and wear wooden masks daubed with animal blood. The tradition originated with the Šokci, a Slavic tribe who migrated to the area, and is said to represent activities intended to frighten away Turkish invaders. Where original participants carried carved and bloodied representations of Turks' heads on their tridents, modern Busós carry tridents with pastries on the end. The festival ends with dancing around a bonfire and burning a straw man effigy.

Busó costumes in Mohács Busójárás museum

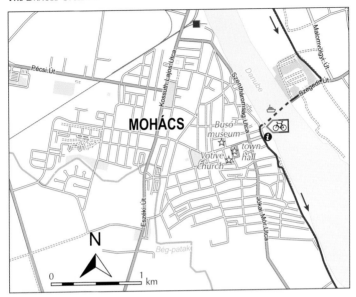

Mohács town hall is built in oriental style

STAGE 6
Mohács to Osijek

Start	Mohács, ferry ramp (86m)
Finish	Osijek, Pješački bridge (79m)
Distance	81km; alternative route 84.5km
Waymarking	Hungary EV6, Croatia Ruta Dunav

Soon after leaving Mohács, the route crosses the border into Croatia and enters Baranja county, an important wine-growing region that suffered badly during the Yugoslav Civil War. This long stage is mostly on quiet country roads and is flat apart from crossing the Bansko Brdo ridge before Batina. An alternative route allows you to follow gravel tracks through the Kopački rit nature reserve.

From top of ferry ramp in **Mohács**, turn L (Szent János utca). Where road turns R into centre of town, continue ahead past restored former silk mill L. Continue into Szabadság tér and fork L onto flood dyke opposite house 1.

After 6km, fork R off dyke (sp Kölked), then turn L at T-junction onto quiet road into **Kölked** (7.5km, 85m).

Continue through village on II Lajos utca, becoming Rózsa utca, back into open country. At junction with main road, turn L (route 56, cycle track R) and follow this road south passing side road to Sátorhely R where cycle track ends. To reach the monument and visitor centre at Mohács battlefield turn right and continue for 1.5km.

THE BATTLE OF MOHÁCS

The first Battle of Mohács (1526), fought between Hungary and the Ottoman Turks, is seen as a watershed in Hungarian history, marking the end of the independent Kingdom of Hungary and the beginning of 160 years of Turkish occupation. In 1525 the Ottoman Turks, who had long held ambitions to extend their territories across the Balkans into central Europe, formed an alliance with France aimed at confronting the power of the Habsburg dominated Holy Roman Empire. Having taken Belgrade (1521), then a Hungarian

The visitor centre at Mohács battlefield site

city, the Turks were well placed to march upon the Habsburg capital Vienna. To do so they had first to conquer Hungary. In 1526 the advancing Turks were confronted by Hungarian troops at Mohács. Sultan Suleiman the Magnificent's army of 100,000 Ottoman troops, including 35,000 mounted cavalry, was opposed by 25,000 Hungarians led by King Ladislaus II. Unsurprisingly, the Hungarian army was routed, with 16,000 soldiers killed or captured. The King, in full armour, managed to escape but drowned when thrown by his horse while crossing a river. Sultan Suleiman's army went on to capture most of Hungary and lay siege to Vienna in 1529, although they failed to capture it. The death of Ladislaus, who had no heir, marked the end of the independent Hungarian Kingdom, the crown passing by marriage to the Austrian Habsburgs, who ruled what was left of the country from Pressburg (modern day Bratislava).

Nearly 160 years later the Turks made another attempt to capture Vienna when, in 1683, they were heavily defeated by the combined forces of the Habsburg controlled Holy Roman Empire and the Kingdom of Poland. Charles of Lorraine, commander of the Habsburg forces, pursued the Turks south into Hungary and in 1687 defeated them again at the second Battle of Mohács (actually at Nagyharsány, 25km south-west). The following year, defeat in Belgrade led to the final expulsion of the Turks from Hungary and the start of Habsburg hegemony, which was to last until 1919.

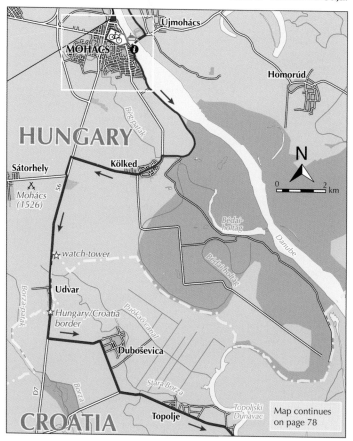

Continue on main road (no cycle lane), passing an old Iron Curtain watch-tower in field L, to reach Hungarian/Croatian border at **Udvar** (17km, 88m). Pass through border checkpoints into Hvratska (Croatia) and after 1km turn L on side road (sp Duboševica). Pass cemetery L to reach crossroads on edge of **Duboševica** (20.5km, 85m) with view of large parish church ahead. Do not enter village, rather turn R at crossroads before village and pass football ground L. Continue through open country to reach T-junction by roadside cross. Turn L and continue on Ulica Republike through **Topolje** (25km, 88m).

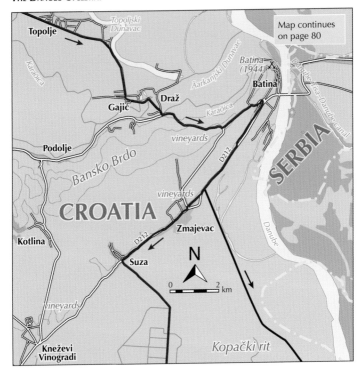

Map continues
on page 80

After village, pass little St Peter and St Paul church behind trees L then follow road for short distance beside **Topoljski Dunavac** Danube backwater. Continue between fields into **Gajić** (30km, 84m) (accommodation).

Follow road (Ulica Matije Gupca) as it bears L in middle of village. Continue over drainage canal and round hairpin bend R to pass through edge of **Draž** (31.5km, 83m) (accommodation, refreshments).

After village, cross another drainage canal and turn L at T-junction. Road soon starts ascending for 1km over wooded Bansko Brdo ridge, reaching 153m at summit. Continue along ridge top through orchards and vineyards for 3km, bearing L at road junction then descending on cobbles to beginning of **Batina** (36.5km, 85m) (accommodation, refreshments). At the top of the main descent, a road L continues along the ridge for 2km to reach Batina Battle monument.

Batina (pop. 500) is a sleepy village tucked between the Danube and the Bansko Brdo ridge. Severely damaged during the Yugoslav Civil War (1991–1995), when much of the population was evacuated, it now boasts a new bridge across the river to Serbia and a new quay on the riverbank. On top of the ridge, with extensive views, is a memorial commemorating the Battle of Batina (1944) fought between the advancing Soviet army and German troops. The Soviets succeeded in establishing a bridgehead across the river but at the expense of 2000 lives, 1279 of whom are buried in a mass grave on the hill. Older residents say the river flowed red with the blood of dead soldiers. The monument, in socialist/realist style, consists of a 27m column topped by an 8m bronze statue of Victory. Just south of the village, on the edge of the Danube, is Zeleni otok (Green island), a recreational and fishing area with guest house and restaurant connected to the mainland by a small bridge.

At bottom of hill turn sharply R taking first exit at roundabout (Ulica Košut Lajoša, sp Kneževi Vinogradi) onto narrow road heading out of village. Continue parallel with main road L for 2km then where narrow road ends continue along main road. After another 2km you reach a point where cycle track R restarts parallel with main road.

Off-road alternative via Kopački rit

Opposite point where cycle track restarts is L turn for alternative route along Danube flood dyke. This option follows good quality gravel tracks along flood dyke which wanders for 29km through swampland of **Kopački rit** nature reserve to rejoin main route before **Kopačevo**. If you take this route make sure you have a supply of insect repellent.

The 17,000ha **Kopački rit** nature reserve is an area of low lying wetland between the Danube and Drava rivers. Captured by Serbia during the civil war, the area was heavily mined. While mine clearance has been undertaken, some areas are still regarded as too dangerous to stray off the paths. After the war it was handed over to the UN before becoming part of Croatia. The Croatian government is developing the reserve as an area for eco-tourism. Several old hunting lodges lie within the park, some of which have been opened up to provide visitor accommodation. There are 40 species of fish spawning in the many lakes and water courses and the reserve is a popular place for anglers seeking giant catfish. Bird species include three kinds of heron, egrets, cormorants and fish eagles; while during spring and autumn it is a stopping off point for many migratory birds. Animals include

large numbers of red deer, wild boar and hares that can often be seen crossing the tracks traversing the reserve. Beavers have built lodges in some of
the lakes.

Main route to Kopačevo

Take cycle track and follow section of old road (Dunavska ulica) for 1km to
roundabout at beginning of **Zmajevac** (42km, 87m) (accommodation). Route
passes below south-east facing slopes of Bansko Brdo ridge. Go straight ahead
at roundabout into Ulica Marsala Tita, winding through village, and continue
through vineyards to reach **Suza** (45km 89m) (accommodation, refreshments,
camping).

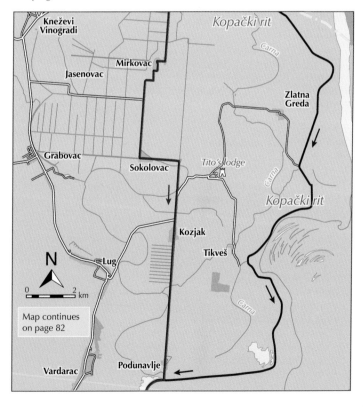

Turn L (Željeznička ulica, sp Mirkovac) in middle of village, then descend over main irrigation canal and continue ahead through fields, eventually bearing R into **Mirkovac** (51.5km, 79m). Turn L in village opposite bus shelter. Pass large former grain warehouse L, then zig-zag R and L, then R and L again, back into open country. Turn L through **Sokolovac** passing intensive poultry farm R, then follow road bearing R at T-junction. Pass turn-off L that leads to Tikveš dvorac. Tikveš dvorac, a former royal hunting lodge that was used by Josip Tito as a country retreat, is being converted into a luxury hotel. Where road bears R towards Lug, fork L (sp Kozjak) and pass through **Kozjak** to reach **Podunavlje** (65.5km, 81m) (refreshments).

After village climb onto flood dyke and turn R. This is where route via Kopački rit rejoins. Follow winding road along flood dyke past Kopački rit visitor centre L (refreshments) and pass **Kopačevo** L (70.5km, 83m) (refreshments, camping). Turn R at T-junction (sp Bilje) then L at triangular junction (sp Osijek) into beginning of Bilje.

Pass palace built as a hunting lodge by Prince Eugene of Savoy behind trees in park R and continue on Ulica Šandora Petefila into centre of **Bilje** (73.5km, 84m) (accommodation, refreshments, tourist office). Go straight ahead at roundabout (Crkvena, second exit) passing church L. Turn L at T-junction (Blatna ulica) and continue through residential area. Follow cycle lane across main road and turn R to leave village across bridge over **Stara Drava** branch of river Drava (cycle track L). Continue beside road, eventually passing behind former filling station, and cross railway passing **Podravlje** L.

Tvrđa fortress was built by the Habsburgs after reconquering Osijek in 1687

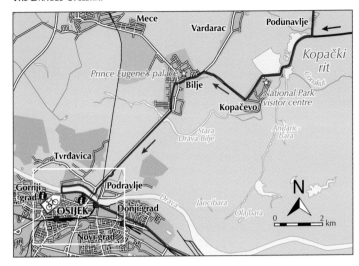

Where road starts to climb towards bridge over Drava, fork half L following cycle track towards river and follow this curving R to pass under bridge. Continue ahead on cycle track beside Drava river, passing between Blagajna beach L and Copacabana water sports complex R (refreshments). Turn L over Drava on Pješački most cyclist suspension bridge into **Osijek** (81km, 79m) (accommodation, refreshments, tourist office, cycle shop, station). Stage ends at end of bridge.

OSIJEK

Osijek (pop. 97,000), which sits beside the River Drava 25km above its confluence with the Danube, is the capital of the Croatian region of Slavonia. The first major settlement on this site was Roman Mursa, an important military and administrative centre that was built on a rise beside the Drava and controlled a stone bridge over the river. It was destroyed by the Huns in AD441. Much later a small medieval town grew which fell to the Ottoman Turks in 1526. The most impressive construction during the Turkish occupation was an 8km long wooden bridge over the Drava and its floodplain, constructed in a few weeks by 25,000 people. Sadly it no longer exists. After ousting the Turks in 1687, the Austrian Habsburgs built a huge new baroque style fortress, Tvrđa, with five bastions that surrounded the old town. At its heart is Trg Svetog Trojstva (Holy Trinity Square), surrounded by important military and civil buildings, with a plague column from 1729 in the centre. The civilian residents were moved to a new upper town (Gornji grad), 1.5km upriver, and here you will find the neo-Gothic cathedral, town hall and main square. Another new town (Donji grad) was built 1.5km downriver to house settlers moving to the area. All three settlements merged to form Osijek (1786) and subsequent infilling and expansion have masked their origins.

During the 20th century Osijek became an important industrial city, the oil refinery in particular being a target for heavy Allied bombing during the Second World War. Other industries include the production of detergents, soap and cosmetics, refining of sugar beet and a brewery. Osijek held out against an attack by Serbian forces of the Yugoslav National Army during the civil war (1991–1995) when it is estimated that 6000 shells landed in the city. Many residents fled, with those remaining sleeping in bomb shelters. Most of the damaged buildings have now been restored. About 800 people were killed by Serbian shelling and airstrikes; while atrocities against Serbs by Croatian forces have led to five Croats, including the Croatian commander General Glavaš, being imprisoned for war crimes.

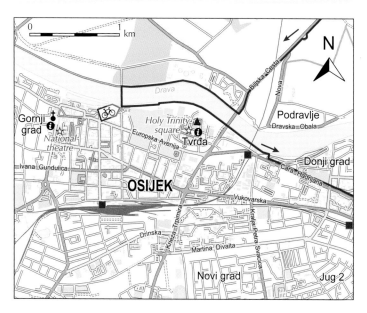

STAGE 7
Osijek to Vukovar

Start	Osijek, Pješački bridge (79m)
Finish	Vukovar, Vuka bridge (81m)
Distance	44.5km
Waymarking	Ruta Dunav EV6

A stage almost entirely on roads, at first following the Drava then crossing a ridge before dropping down to reach the Danube. This area was a heavily fought over front line during the Yugoslav Civil War and signs warning of possible landmines and unexploded ordinance should be obeyed. The stage is flat apart from a ridge crossed between Bijelo Brdo and Dalj.

From S end of Pješački bridge in **Osijek**, cycle E on cycle track beside Drava, passing **Tvrđa** fortress R. Pass under road and railway bridges, then just before reaching small dock, turn R away from river to reach main road. Turn L (Ulica

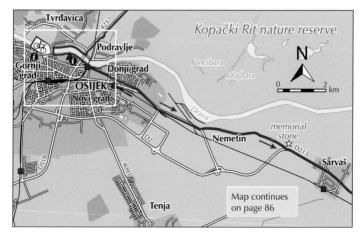

Map continues on page 86

Memorial to 714 Croat survivors of Serbian concentration camps near Nemetin

cara Hadrijana) on cycle track L of wide boulevard with tram tracks beside road. Continue ahead at turn-off to Donji Grad, which you pass L. Main road becomes Matije Gupca and reaches tram turning circle where cycle track ends. Cross to R of road and continue ahead on main road (no cycle lane at first) passing through industrial area (where cycle track reappears) into open country. Cross railway crossing and 100 metres after filling station L fork L on side road through small settlement of **Nemetin** (6.5km, 85m).

Continue through village to reach T-junction with memorial stone to 714 victims of Yugoslav Civil War L. Turn L and join cycle lane L that leads to **Sarvaš** (13km, 90m) (station) and on through next village **Bijelo Brdo** (16km, 90m) (accommodation, refreshments, station).

Soon after village, road climbs steadily for 1.5km over small ridge, then descends gently for 5km. Towards bottom of hill, turn R on track that crosses railway by Dalj station. Continue ahead on Ulica Bana Josipa Jelačića to reach centre of **Dalj** (26km, 83m) (accommodation, refreshments, station), a village beside Danube.

Bear R in front of church. After 1km follow road bearing L out of village into open country and continue straight between fields for 7km to reach strung out village of **Borovo**.

Turn R beside house 131 (Ulica Petra Kolčića) into quiet residential street, then L (Ulica Đorđa Sremca). Go ahead (Ratarska ulica) over series of crossroads, then follow road bearing R and L beside old railway line R. Go ahead (Ulica Jana Bate) over main road and continue between Danube L and railway R. This was the front line in the Yugoslav Civil War where ruined buildings now alternate with modern post-war reconstruction. Bear L at T-junction (Kolodvorska Ulica), then follow road bending R and cross railway level crossing. Bear R beside railway, then turn first L and continue over two crossroads to reach roundabout in **Borovo Naselje** (40km, 86m) (accommodation, refreshments, station).

Turn L (Priljevo ulica, second exit) and join cycle track R. Go ahead at second roundabout and continue past Vukovar port and ruined Vukovar railway station (both L). Cross bridge over railway and turn R at roundabout (Ulica Ivana Gundulića, first exit) into one-way system. Continue into Kardinala Alojzija Stepinca to reach bridge over river Vuka in centre of **Vukovar** (44.5km, 81m) (accommodation, refreshments, tourist office, cycle shop, station).

VUKOVAR

Vukovar (pop. 23,000, but was 46,000 before civil war) was a small medieval trading town that suffered serious depopulation during the Turkish occupation (1526–1687) when the indigenous Croat and Hungarian inhabitants either fled or were slaughtered. When the Turks were expelled by the Habsburgs, the almost empty land was repopulated by a mixture of nationalities including Germans, Slovaks, Ukrainians and Russians, in addition to returning Croats and Hungarians, thus establishing a situation that would contribute to the disaster which occurred some 300 years later. The land around Vukovar became the property of Philip Eltz, Archbishop of Mainz (a close ally of the Habsburg emperor) who built Eltz palace as his residence in the town. The town lived mainly by agricultural and craft industries. The vast Eltz estate remained in family hands until 1945 when the German inhabitants (about one third of the population) were expelled and replaced by Yugoslav Serbs, Bosnians and Montenegrins. Incidentally, Jakob Eltz, the heir to the estate, returned to Vukovar after the secession of Croatia from Yugoslavia, took Croatian nationality, became a member of the Croatian parliament and fought in the civil war defending the city.

Following the creation of Yugoslavia (1919), industrial development began which accelerated after the communists took control in 1945. This industrialisation attracted workers from all over Yugoslavia with the population expanding to reach 46,000 by 1991. Indigenous Croats perceived themselves to be marginalised as more power was concentrated in Yugoslav (mostly Serb) hands. When the Yugoslav Civil War broke out between Croatia and Serbia in 1991, Vukovar was on the front line. Battle for control of the city lasted 87 days and it is estimated that Yugoslav and Serb forces fired up to 12,000 shells and rockets into the city per day, making it the fiercest European battle since the Second World War. The city was completely destroyed and most of the population fled, many never to return. Post-war recovery has been slow and Vukovar remains an ethnically divided city where approximately equal numbers of Croats and Serbs remain wary of each other's actions and intentions. Before the war Vukovar was a thriving baroque city with attractive churches, civil buildings and the Eltz palace. Now it is a mix of restored buildings, modern glass and concrete structures and untouched ruins, the most poignant being the shell-marked and battered water tower that has been preserved as a symbol of the conflict.

STAGE 8
Vukovar to Bačka Palanka

Start	Vukovar, Vuka bridge (81m)
Finish	Bačka Palanka, St John the Baptist church (81m)
Distance	40.5km
Waymarking	Ruta Dunav EV6

This stage, all on quiet roads along the edge of a plateau beside the Danube valley, which is 30m below, is the most strenuous stage so far. The road descends, four times, steeply down to river level and climbs back equally steeply. Towards the end, Croatia is left behind and the Danube is crossed by bridge to reach the Serbian town of Bačka Palanka.

Ruined water tower in Vukovar, preserved as a memorial to the Yugoslav Civil War

From Vuka river bridge in centre of **Vukovar**, cycle south ascending steadily on Frankopanska ulica, which becomes Ulica Nikole Andrića then, after road joins from L, Ulica Stjepana Radića. Where road curves L, join cycle track R and continue past shell damaged **water tower**, symbol of post-civil war Vukovar L. Soon after, gradient levels out and road continues straight ahead through suburbs and into open country. You are now on top of an elevated plateau about 30m above the Danube, although neither river nor riverside cliffs are visible. Pass extensive **Vukovar war cemetery** R, where cycle track ends, and road L leading to **Vučedol archaeological site**.

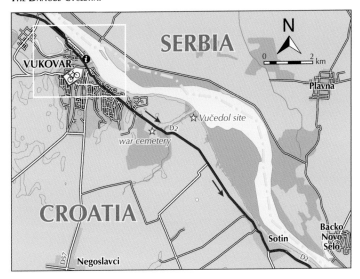

The **Vučedol** culture started around 3000BC and by 2200BC had spread to cover most of modern day Croatia, Bosnia, Serbia, Hungary and Slovakia. It is seen as the precursor to the Bronze Age in Europe as it used a novel method of smelting copper to make everyday tools. The most famous discovery at Vučedol is a ceramic 'dove' shaped vessel, now believed to be a fertility symbol in the shape of a partridge. Some 3000 inhabitants occupied the site, on the banks of the Danube. It was badly damaged during the civil war but has since been restored and is open to visitors (closed Mondays).

Continue close to cliffs L to reach **Sotin** (10km, 109m) (refreshments) perched on cliff top, 30m above Danube. Go straight ahead and near end of village turn L (sp Ilok) following main road towards river. For next 6km road runs through fields parallel with Danube between 200 metres and 500 metres from the cliff top L to reach **Opatovac** (17.5km, 84m) (accommodation, refreshments).

Here road bears L to make first (of four) steep descents 30 metres down into a coombe at river level before bearing R and climbing equally steeply back onto the plateau then continuing along the cliff top to descend again to **Mohovo** (21.5km, 84m).

Climb back to cliff top and continue level for 6km before descending again into **Šarengrad** (27.5km, 81m) (accommodation, refreshments, camping). This time the road runs through the village close to the Danube before climbing less steeply up to the plateau. After 2km you descend again, this time into an uninhabited coombe. After regaining the plateau it is a short cycle to **Ilok** (35km, 132m) (accommodation, refreshments, tourist office, cycle shop).

Ilok (pop. 4000, but 7000 in 1991), the most easterly town in Croatia, was an administrative and military centre during the Turkish occupation and some elements of Turkish architecture remain. The castle, on a hill overlooking the Danube, was restored after the occupation with wine cellars cut into the hill beneath. These are used to store large quantities of locally grown Traminer and Riesling wine. During the civil war, the town's exposed position (surrounded on three sides by Serbian territory) led the Croat population to flee and the Yugoslav army captured it with minimal damage.

Cycle through town centre on Ulica Dr Franje Tuđmana and after passing town hall and library L start descending (road now called Koševi ulica, becoming Ulica Stjepana Radića, then Ulica Julija Benešića) dropping down (for last time) to river level. Pass L turn leading to old ferry and instead bear R on Ulica Ivana Gorana Kovačića. Just before end of built-up area, turn L on slip road leading to Danube bridge and turn L onto bridge approach to reach **Croatian border post**.

Map continues on page 92

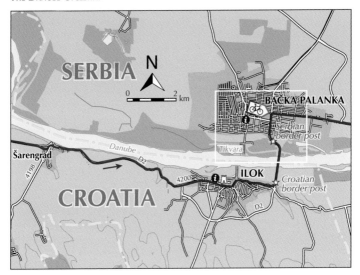

Continue across bridge to reach **Serbian border post**. Keep ahead on main road (Svetozara Miletića) [Светозара Милетића] into built-up area to reach **St John the Baptist Orthodox church** R on corner of third crossroads in **Bačka Palanka** [Бачка Паланка] (40.5km, 81m) (accommodation, refreshments, camping, tourist office, cycle shop).Turn L (Kralja Petra I) [Краља Петра I] to reach the town centre or R to continue on Stage 9.

> **Bačka Palanka** (pop. 29,000) is an amalgam of three towns, Stara Palanka (Old Palanka, mostly Serbs who had survived Turkish occupation), Nova Palanka (New Palanka, new Serb settlers after the occupation) and Nemačka Palanka (German Palanka, new German settlers after the occupation). By the time they merged in the 20th century there was an overall German majority. In 1945 the German population was expelled and the city repopulated with ethnic Serbs from Bosnia. During the civil war, 5000 Serb refugees arrived from Croatia and Bosnia and many have stayed.

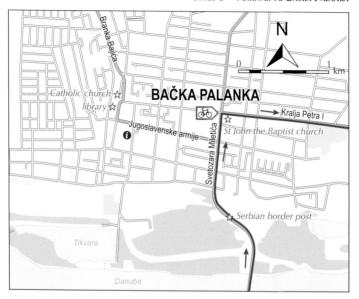

Bačka Palanka library

STAGE 9
Bačka Palanka to Novi Sad

Start	Bačka Palanka, St John the Baptist church (81m)
Finish	Novi Sad, Varadinski bridge (79m)
Distance	43.5km
Waymarking	Dunavska ruta EV6

This stage crosses the Serbian autonomous region of Vojvodina, at first on a busy main road but then joining the Danube flood dyke, which is followed right into the centre of Serbia's second city, Novi Sad. This is another completely flat stage.

From crossroads beside **St John the Baptist church** in Bačka Palanka, cycle east along Kralja Petra I [Краља Петра I] following this street straight for 2km out of city and past modern industrial units. At end of town continue ahead on main road (route 7) for 6km to reach road junction. Follow route 7 forking R to by-pass **Čelarevo** [Челарево] L (11km, 76m). Home of Serbia's second largest brewery, Lav Pivo (owned by Carlsberg); there is a beer museum and a visitor centre.

After 2km, just before 143km post, turn R at road junction (sp Futog) beside industrial area, then fork R on side road leading to Danube. Turn L along flood dyke on quiet road with riverside cabins R. Continue for 7.5km, first beside river but eventually bearing L beside woodland to reach fishing lake near Begeč. Turn sharply R beside lake and continue along flood dyke to reach T-junction. Turn L, still following flood dyke. After 1.5km, pass turn-off for **Begeč** [Бегеч] (22km, 78m) (accommodation), which can be seen L.

Continue on flood dyke between fields L and wooded swampland R to pass **Futog** [Футог] (28km, 79m) (accommodation, refreshments, cycle shop, station) with distant views of Fruška Gora mountains across river R. Beyond village pass aggregates quay R and join cycle track L of road passing **Veternik** [Ветерничка] (34km, 76m) (accommodation, refreshments).

Built-up area of Veternik merges indistinctly into that of Novi Sad. A considerable number of executive houses have been built on R, between the flood dyke and Danube. Where road bears L, fork R on asphalt cycle track along flood dyke. Where this track ends, fork R through barrier and immediately turn L onto cobbled street and R at T-junction (Kaplara) [каплара] still cobbled. The fenced-off area to the R is a Serbian naval base. Continue on to asphalt road past Soviet era housing blocks R, and turn R at T-junction (Balzakova) [Балзакова] on cycle track R. Bear L at end into Bulevar Despota Stefana [Булевар Деспота Стефана], passing nightclub R with rear half of helicopter sticking out into street. Join cycle track R and continue under Slobode most [Слободе мост] Danube road bridge. Slobode bridge is a new bridge rebuilt after NATO bombing destroyed all bridges over the Danube in Novi Sad.

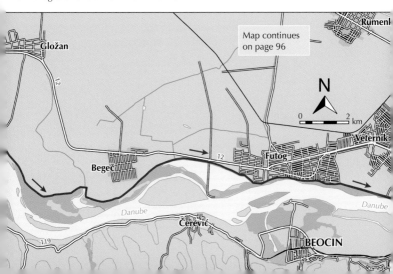

This Soviet era helicopter ended up as part of a nightclub in Novi Sad

Continue ahead for 250m then turn R beside bus turning circle. Ascend onto flood dyke and turn L along riverside promenade (Sunčani Kay) [Сунчани Кеј] with view of Petrovaradin [Петроварадик] **fortress** across river R. Just before Varadinski bridge [Варадински мост] turn L, climbing up onto bridge approach road. Turn R over bridge to continue on Stage 10, or L (Bulevar Mihajla Pupina) [Булевар Михајла Пупина] to reach centre of **Novi Sad** [Нови Сад] (43.5km, 79m) (accommodation, YH, refreshments, tourist office, cycle shop, station).

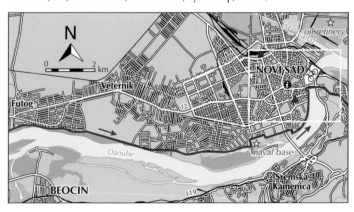

The Name of Mary Catholic cathedral in Novi Sad

NOVI SAD

Novi Sad (pop. 215,000) is the capital of Vojvodina and the second largest city in Serbia. Prior to the Habsburg expulsion of Ottoman Turks (1687), the only development was on the right bank of the Danube at Petrovaradin (see next stage). The Austrians forbade non-Catholics from residing in Petrovaradin, leading to the establishment in 1694 of Novi Sad (which translates as 'new plantation') as a Serbian Orthodox settlement on the opposite bank. It grew steadily and by 1817 was the largest Serb municipality in the world. During the 1848 revolution against Habsburg domination, Novi Sad was heavily bombarded across the river by Austrian troops garrisoned in Petrovaradin, destroying much of the city and causing the population to fall from 17,000 (1843) to 7000 (1850). A post-revolution policy of repopulating the city with Hungarians and Germans meant that by 1870 the Serbs were a minority. Expulsion of many Hungarians after the First World War and of Germans after the Second resulted in the city returning to its predominantly Serb roots by 1950. Rapid post-war industrialisation more than doubled the population to 180,000 (1991) and an influx of 50,000 Serb refugees from Bosnia and Croatia during the civil war expanded the population still further. NATO reprisal bombing raids during the Kosovo campaign (1999) destroyed all three bridges and severely damaged the city.

The devastation of 1848 has led to the city having very few pre-19th-century buildings. Main sights, mostly in Stari grad (old town), are the two cathedrals of St George (Orthodox) and Name of Mary (Catholic), the City Hall in Trg Slobode square [Трг Слободе] and the Serbian National theatre. The core city is surrounded by communist era housing developments linked by wide boulevards.

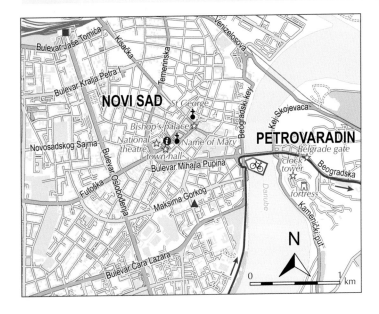

STAGE 10
Novi Sad to Novi Slankamen

Start	Novi Sad, Varadinski bridge (79m)
Finish	Novi Slankamen, crossroads (146m)
Distance	41km
Waymarking	Dunavska ruta EV6

Crossing to the right (south) bank of the Danube, the route climbs out of Petrovaradin then undulates through the foothills of the Fruška Gora mountains. After Beška the route becomes level and crosses an agricultural plateau to Novi Slankamen, 60 metres above and 1.5km from the riverside village of Stari Slankamen.

From western end of Varadinski bridge [Варадински мост] in **Novi Sad**, cycle east across bridge. Pass entrance to **Petrovaradin fortress** R and continue on Beogradska [Београдска] through **Belgrade gate** into **Petrovaradin** [Петроварадин] (accommodation, refreshments, station).

PETROVARADIN FORTRESS

Petrovaradin fortress, which played a decisive role in the 17th-century struggle between Habsburg Austrians and Ottoman Turks for control over the region, dominates a bluff overlooking the Danube. The hill had already hosted Palaeolithic, Neolithic and Bronze Age settlements before the Romans built a fort (Cusum) on this hill as part of their Danube fortifications. A monastery built by Hungarians (1247) was later fortified to defend it against Turkish invaders, but it fell to the Turks in 1526. After Habsburg liberation (1687), the Austrians strengthened the fortress sufficiently for it to survive two Turkish attacks, first in 1694 and again in 1716 when 76,000 Austrian troops defeated 150,000 Turks in a battle that proved to be the end of the Turkish threat to central Europe.

The current shape of the fortress dates from 1751–1776, when the old fortifications were pulled down and replaced with an impressive new above-ground structure matched by four levels of underground bunkers and 16km of tunnels. These never saw action against the Turks, although they were used against Hungarian revolutionaries in the 1848 uprising against Habsburg domination. After the First World War, when Yugoslav authorities ordered the destruction of all the old Austrian fortresses in the country because they had lost their military significance, Petrovaradin survived because it was a beautiful edifice. The clock tower, one of Novi Sad's principal landmarks, has a clock with reversed hands, with the small hand indicating minutes and the larger one, which can be seen from a greater distance, showing hours. In recent years the fortress has hosted EXIT, the largest annual pop music festival in south-eastern Europe.

The clock on Petrovaradin fortress has a large hour hand and small minute hand

Continue through town on Preradoviceva [Прерадовићева] and follow main road forking L (sp Beograd) at first ascending gently into open country then descending. At beginning of built-up area, fork R uphill off main road onto Petrovaradinska [Петроварадинска]. Descend round hairpin bends into Patrijarha Rajačiča [Патријарха Рајачића] to reach centre of **Sremski Karlovci** [Сремски Карловци] (9km, 86m) (accommodation, refreshments, tourist office, station).

Sremski Karlovci (pop. 8800) was unusual in maintaining its Serbian Orthodox population during the Turkish occupation, becoming the largest Serbian town in Turkish hands. After liberation, the treaty ending hostilities between Ottoman and Habsburg empires was signed in Karlowitz, as the city was known in German. Although now in Habsburg controlled Hungary, it retained its Serbian majority and became the seat of the Orthodox Patriarch of Serbia (the leader of the Serbian church) and the spiritual capital for Serbs throughout the Austro-Hungarian Empire. The Italianate style Patriarch's Court is still the administrative headquarters of the Serbian church and also houses a treasury of valuable relics rescued from abandoned Orthodox churches in Bosnia and Croatia. The symbol of Sremski Karlovci is the Four Lions fountain, a red marble structure installed to commemorate the town's first waterworks in 1799.

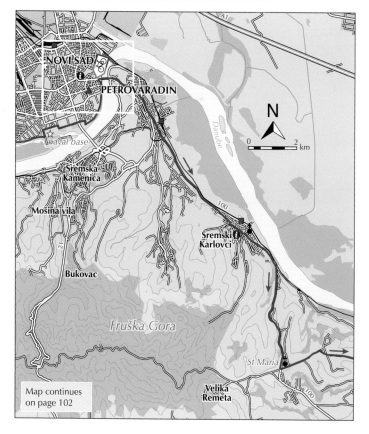

Map continues on page 102

*Patriarch's court in Sremski Karlovci is the
headquarters of the Serbian Orthodox church*

Bear R by Four Lions fountain in main square, with Patriarch's court palace entrance L, then turn L between Catholic church L and old gimnazija grammar school R, into Mitropolita Stratimirovića [Митрополита Стратимировића]. Follow this street out of town, bearing R onto main road at end of built-up area.

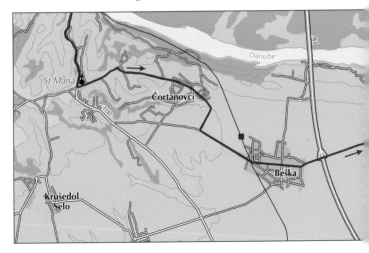

The forested line of hills rising to the south are the **Fruška Gora** mountains that have been a nature reserve since 1960. In the valleys between the mountains are 16 Orthodox abbeys, some of them dating from the period of the Ottoman occupation when Christians fled from the towns into the countryside. The TV tower still shows damage from NATO bombing aimed at deterring Serbian attacks upon Kosovo (1999). The lower slopes are covered with vineyards producing high quality wine from riesling, traminer and frankovca grapes.

Follow main road climbing steadily for 4km to reach crossroads at top of hill (15.5km, 270m). Turn L beside cream coloured St Maria church with green and gold domes that sparkle in the sun then descend through Banstol [Банстол] using cycle lane R into **Čortanovci** [Чортановци] (20km, 158m) (accommodation, camping).

Fork L (sp Beška) and continue through village, then fork R downhill, go ahead over crossroads and follow road ahead uphill through fields. At top of hill, bear L and continue downhill between fields. Fork R to pass under railway on cycle track and bear L beside blue water tower on Kralja Petra I [Краља Петра I] into **Beška** [Бешка] (26.5km, 120m) (accommodation, refreshments, station). Railway is high-speed line from Belgrade to Budapest via Novi Sad.

Continue through town on Kneza Miloša [Кнеза Милоша] into open country. Cross motorway and continue on main road through fields to **Krčedin** [Крчедин] (31.5km, 112m) (refreshments).

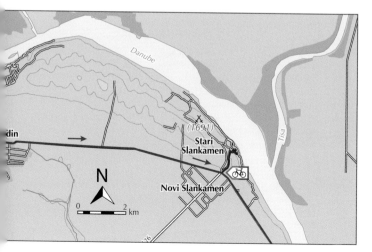

Riverside marina and restaurant at Stari Slankamen

Pass through village and continue on road through fields and orchards, then keep L at fork to reach crossroads (refreshments) on edge of **Novi Slankamen** [Нови Сланкамен] (41km, 146m). (To reach **Stari Slankamen** [Стари Сланкамен] (1.5km, 83m) (accommodation, refreshments), turn L on Cara Dušana [Цара Душана] and descend steeply on cobbled road round hairpin bends to riverbank).

Before 1992, **Novi Slankamen** (pop. 3200) was a Croat majority village in Serbian territory. The Croats were forced to leave during the civil war and replaced with displaced Serbs from Croatia and Bosnia. **Stari Slankamen** (pop. 675), positioned opposite the confluence of the river Tisa, was the site of a Roman camp (Acumincum) and later a medieval fortified town. In 1691, the final battle of the Great Turkish War between the Turkish Ottoman and Austrian Habsburg Empires was fought here. Victory for the Habsburgs led eventually to the Treaty of Karlowitz. A 16m obelisk commemorates the battle.

STAGE 11
Novi Slankamen to Belgrade

Start	Novi Slankamen, crossroads (146m)
Finish	Belgrade, St Alexander Nevsky church, Dorćol (82m)
Distance	53km
Waymarking	Dunavska ruta EV6

After descending steadily for 20km on a road between fields, the dormitory towns of Banovci and Batajnica soon give way to the suburban built-up sprawl of greater Belgrade. The roads, quiet at first, become increasingly busy nearing the city. The final leg is on asphalt riverside cycle tracks through urban parkland. There are some gentle ascents and descents, but no steep climbs.

Follow road heading south-east from crossroads between **Novi Slankamen** and **Stari Slankamen**, descending steadily past swimming pool complex at Bazeni Horizont L through arable fields to reach **Surduk** [Сурдук] (9km, 105m) (refreshments). Continue on straight road between fields and turn R at T-junction on Kralja Petra I [Краља Петра I] to reach St Nicholas church in centre of **Belegiš** [Белегиш] (15km, 97m) (refreshments).

Pass through village, joining cycle track L which continues through open country into **Stari Banovci** [Стари Бановци] (refreshments). Stari Banovci, Banovci Dunav and Novi Banovci make up one continuous built-up area. Where cycle track ends, turn L on Stevna Tišme [Стевна Тишме] and first R on Grčka [Грчка]. At end, bear R to reach main road and turn L on Milenka Pevca [Миленка Певца], uphill into **Banovci Dunav** [Бановци Дунав] (23km, 89m) (accommodation, refreshments).

Continue on Svetosavska [Светосавска] through **Novi Banovci** [Нови Бановци] (accommodation, refreshments). At end of built-up area cross motorway then go ahead over roundabout (second exit sp Batajnica). Continue gently downhill through open country with military airfield R to reach beginning of another built-up area. Follow Jovana Brankovića [Јована Бранковића] into **Batajnica** [Батајница] (30km, 77m) (accommodation, refreshments, cycle shop, station).

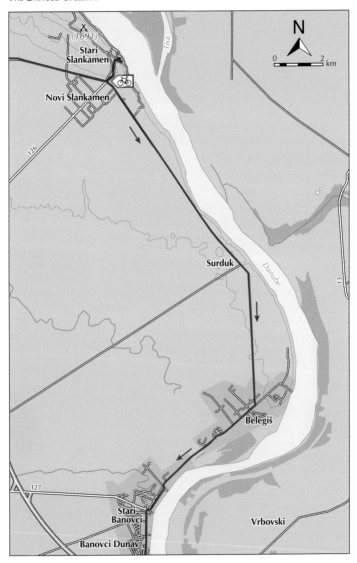

Batajnica (pop. 35,000) is a fast growing dormitory town for Belgrade. The nearby military airfield, which is now an important base for the Serbian and former Yugoslav air force, was heavily bombed by NATO forces during the Yugoslav Civil War.

Turn L beside house 90 (Sava Grkinića) [Саве Гркинића] and continue into Vojvodanskih Brigada [војвођанских Бригада]. At end bear R (Makisma Brankovića) [Максима Бранковића] then dog-leg R and L over staggered cross-roads to reach traffic lights. Turn L and follow Majora Zorana Radosavljevića [Мајора Зорана Радосављевића] out of town.

At end of Batajnica, pass under motorway and follow main road for 10km through open country L and a never-ending series of small industrial developments R. The road from Batajnica to Zemun is a busy main road with no cycle lane. Go straight ahead at major road junction (Cara Dušana) [Цара Душана] and after 600 metres (opposite building 149 R), turn L onto side road (Ulica Dr Mušickog) [Улица Др Мушиког]. Turn R at T-junction (Ulica Pregrevica) [Улица Прегревица], with Danube behind houses L, and continue ahead into Despota Đurđa [Деспота Ђурђа]. Pass viewpoint over Danube L and follow street bearing R, L and R again to reach T-junction. Turn L beside cemetery (Sibinjanin Janka)

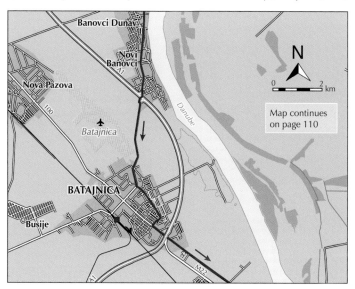

Gardoš tower in Zemun was built to celebrate 1000 years of Hungarian rule

[Сибињанин Jaнка] and continue steeply downhill (Ulica Sinđelićeva) [Улица Синђелићева] on very rough cobbles into **Zemun** [Земун] (43km, 78m) (accommodation, refreshments, camping, cycle shop, station).

Zemun (pop. 156,000) was an independent and ancient city, built on three hills, that has been absorbed into greater Belgrade. As Roman Taurunum it was a harbour for the Roman Danube fleet. During medieval times Zemun was on the Military Frontier between the Hungarian Kingdom (later Habsburg Austria) and the Ottoman Turkish Empire. It remained in Austro-Hungarian hands when nearby Belgrade fell to the Turks in 1813. The opening shots of the First World War were fired here on 29 July 1914, when Austro-Hungarian naval vessels based in Zemun opened fire on Serbian positions in Belgrade across the river Sava. The oldest part of town has narrow cobbled streets and a few ruins of a medieval fortress. The most recognisable symbol of the city, Gardoš tower (1896), an eclectic mix of architectural styles, was built to commemorate 1000 years of Hungarian settlement. There are extensive views of Zemun, Belgrade and the Danube from the tower. Modern Zemun is a prosperous and industrially active part of Belgrade.

At bottom of hill, turn L (Njegoševa) [Његошева] to reach Danube promenade. Turn R on Kej Oslobođenja [Кеј ослобођења], and after 300 metres turn L through car park and R in front of restaurant onto riverside cycle track. Continue through parklands, following branch of Danube past Veliko Ratno Ostrovo island [Велико ратно острво] L into **Novi Beograd** [Нови Београд] (45.5km, 75m) (accommodation, refreshments, cycle shop, station).

In Soviet times, Hotel Jugoslavija in Novi Beograd was the largest hotel in the country

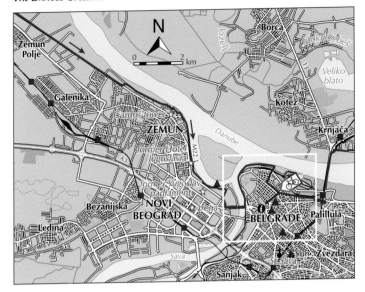

Continue past site of previous **Hotel Jugoslavija** R. Once the largest and most prestigious hotel in Yugoslavia, the Soviet era concrete blockhouse Hotel Jugoslavija was damaged by NATO bombing (1999) and is now being redeveloped as a five-star hotel. Soon after hotel, cycle track branches R from pedestrian footpath and winds its own way through parkland with large concrete Palace of Serbia (formerly the **Yugoslavian parliament building**) R. Where cycle track reaches road, follow cycle track turning R beside road, then at crossroads turn L across road and follow Bvd Nicola Tesla [Булевар Николе Тесле] using cycle track L. Where this reaches main road, turn L and cross river Sava over Brankov most [Бранков мост] bridge.

On far side of bridge (49km) a **cycle lift** L allows you to take your cycle down to river level. The road ahead continues to the city centre though it is very busy and is not recommended for cyclists. The former Austrian gunboat, Sava, now permanently moored beside the bridge, fired the opening bombardment of the First World War, shelling Belgrade from Zemun on 29 July 1914.

Take cycle lift down then turn L away from river and R to follow cycle track ahead beside Sava past cruise boat landing stages L and old warehouses now converted into bars and restaurants R, with **Kalemegdan fortress** rising behind. Continue round point where Sava and Danube join and past large Metropolitain

University **sports centre** with multi-coloured concrete tower R. Continue ahead winding through parkland and where cycle track ends, turn R (Dunavski kej) [Дунавски кej] past apartment buildings R. Dogleg L and R then pass through tunnel under railway and continue into Dubrovačka [Дубровачка]. Turn L beside building 5 into Skender-Begova [СкендерБегова] and follow this for six city blocks, passing tram depot L, to reach stage end at crossroads beside St Alexander Nevsky church [Храм Светог Александра Невског] R in Dorćol [Дорћол] district of Belgrade (53km, 82m).

To reach city centre, turn R (Žorža Klemansoa [Жоржа Клемансоа]) beside church, then go ahead over crossroads (Francuska [Француска]) and cycle steadily uphill for 700m to **Trg Republike square** [Трг Републике] in centre of **Belgrade** [Београд] (53.5km, 112m) (accommodation, refreshments, tourist office, cycle shop, station).

BELGRADE

Belgrade (metro area pop. 1,275,000), known in Serbian as Beograd, is the capital of Serbia and before the country broke up was the largest city and federal capital of Yugoslavia. The city started as a small Celtic settlement on a hill, nowadays the site of the Kalemegdan fortress, overlooking the confluence of the river Sava with the Danube. The Romans, who arrived in 29BC, developed this settlement into the city of Singidunum by expanding along the eastern side of the hill where the regular grid of streets around Studentski park (the site of the forum) follow the original Roman layout. When the Roman Empire split in AD395 the Sava became the border between eastern and western empires leaving Singidunum on the border of the eastern empire. This left it very exposed and over the next 200 years the city was overrun by a succession of barbarian tribes before being completely destroyed by the Avars in the early seventh century.

In the ninth century the Slavs established Beograd ('white city', after the colour of the local building stone) on the site of Singidunum. This changed hands between Byzantine, Frankish, Bulgarian and Hungarian empires before becoming capital of Serbia for the first time in 1282. In 1521 Serbia was captured by the Ottoman Turks, who were themselves defeated by the Habsburg Austrians in 1687. Once again Belgrade found itself on the front line between warring empires with the Austro-Hungarian military frontier north of the Danube and west of the Sava and the Turks to the south and east. Final defeat of the Turks in 1841 led to Belgrade becoming capital of Serbia for the second time. But war was not over and the

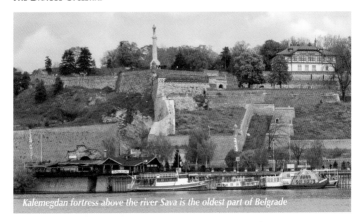

Kalemegdan fortress above the river Sava is the oldest part of Belgrade

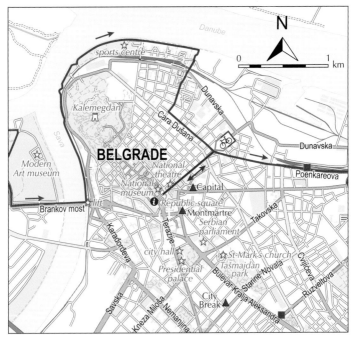

Austro-Hungarians, who remained on the other side of the river, attacked Belgrade in 1914 at the start of the First World War. It is claimed that Belgrade has been fought over in 115 battles and destroyed 44 times. All of this meant that in 1900 the city had a population of only 70,000 and very little in the way of historic buildings.

The Treaty of Trianon in 1919 led to the formation of Yugoslavia with Belgrade as its capital. The population grew rapidly to reach 320,000 by 1940 and the first bridges were built over the rivers Danube and Sava. During the Second World War the city was bombed by both German (1941) and Allied air forces (1944) causing much damage. The post-war communist government instituted a policy of rapid industrialisation and construction of apartment buildings to house workers drawn to the city. This led to the development of a new city, Novi Beograd, built between Belgrade and Zemun, creating one large urban area with a population of 1,130,000 in 1990. The former Yugoslav national parliament and many government and ministerial buildings are in Novi Beograd. During the Yugoslav Civil War, Belgrade was bombed by NATO planes in reprisal raids to counter Serbian military activity in Kosovo causing substantial damage. After the break-up of Yugoslavia, the city became capital of Serbia for a third time.

The city's oldest buildings (indeed the only pre-18th-century buildings) are the upper and lower fortresses in Kalemegdan park. Other important buildings in the city centre include the National museum in Republic square, parliament building, city hall and presidential palace in Nikole Pašića square and St Mark's church in Tašmajdan park. South of the centre on the Vračar hill is St Sava cathedral, the largest Orthodox cathedral in the world. Building began in 1935, but was halted by the Second World War and post-war communist government objections prevented work from restarting until 1985. Although the façade, outside walls and dome are complete the interior is still unfinished. The former bohemian quarter of Skadarlija [Скадарлија] is a narrow street close to Republic square where you will find a number of traditional bars and restaurants.

113

STAGE 12

Belgrade to Kovin

Start	Belgrade, St Alexander Nevsky church, Dorćol (82m)
Finish	Kovin, marina (70m)
Distance	67km; alternative route 56.5km
Waymarking	Dunavska ruta EV6

After following city streets through Belgrade, the route crosses the Danube and follows flood dykes to the industrial city of Pančevo, then quiet country roads and another long stretch on flood dykes to Kovin. The long stretches of flood dyke are mostly unsurfaced; an alternative route is available using asphalt country roads. After Belgrade the route is completely flat.

Between Belgrade and Stara Palanka (Stages 12–13) the official route follows long stretches of unsurfaced track along the top of flood dykes. To avoid these, alternative road routes can be used between Belgrade–Pančevo, Omoljica–Kovin (both Stage 12) and Kovin–Dubovac (Stage 13).

From crossroads beside St Alexander Nevsky church in **Belgrade**, cycle E on Venizelosova [венизелосова]. Continue into Poencareova [Поенкареова] and pass old railway yards L. Turn R uphill beside building 27 and at end turn L (Bvd Despota Stefana [Булевар Деспота СтеФана]). After 100m join R lane, then pass under two bridges and fork R spiralling up to join approach road to Pančevački most [Панчевачки мост] bridge.

Cross bridge over Danube using poor condition cycle track R. At end of bridge fork immediately R on gravel track beside road. Gravel track can only be accessed at the bridge end, after that it is separated behind crash barriers. After 200m, turn R over grass verge onto parallel gravel road and bear L to reach path junction (4.5km, 70m) where there is a choice of routes.

Serbian parliament building in Belgrade

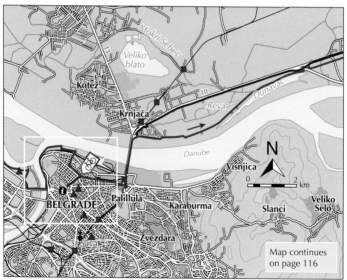

Map continues on page 116

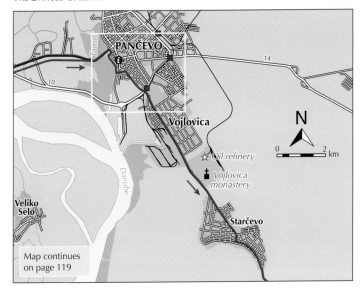

Alternative route avoiding unsurfaced tracks

Keep ahead on gravel road beside main road, then follow this bearing R (Pančevački put) [Панчевачки пут]. Dog-leg R and L around houses, then turn L to reach motorway and R on red asphalt bus and cycle lane beside main carriageway. This is a six lane motorway with dedicated combined bus/cycle lanes in both directions. After 6.5km, follow road forking R which rises to cross motorway and descend to road junction where main route is rejoined.

Main route on unsurfaced flood dykes

Turn R onto gravel track (sp Pančevo) then after 100m, fork R on unsurfaced track parallel with Danube flood dyke. After 1km, dogleg L and R onto Danice Jovanović [Данице Јовановић] between village and flood dyke. Opposite house 17, turn R across concrete slab over stream then follow grassy track L which climbs up onto flood dyke. Follow grassy track along dyke for 7km. Drop down off flood dyke L to pass under motorway, then fork R to regain path along dyke. Continue for 3km, crossing disused asphalt road, to emerge on main road and bear R. This is where alternative route rejoins.

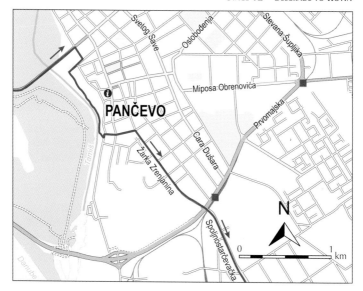

Combined route continues

Continue ahead, then cross river Tamiš and turn R on Trg Mučenika [Трг Мученика] into **Pančevo** [Панчево] (17km, 76m) (accommodation, refreshments, tourist office, cycle shop, station).

> **Pančevo** (pop. 76,000) is an industrial town with an aircraft factory (producing Utva training aircraft) and an oil refinery. As part of the military frontier between Habsburg and Ottoman territory after 1751, it was repopulated with many Swabian (German) and Hungarian settlers, so much so that by 1910 the Serb population was in a minority. Most of the Hungarians left after 1919, while the Germans were expelled after the Second World War.

Turn R (Svetozara Miletića) [Светозара Милетића] and continue through car park towards Tamiš. Turn L on winding cycle track beside river and follow this for 800 metres to reach riverside road. Turn sharply L away from river, then bear R (Milorad Bata) [Милорада Бате] through socialist era housing development. Turn R at second traffic lights (Žarka Zrenjanina) [Жарка Зрењанина] (cycle track R) and follow this through town and across main road junction. Cross railway level crossing and continue into Spoljnostarčevačka [Спољностарчевачка], passing

117

industrial estate R and **oil refinery** L. There is a barely useable cycle track beside the road R from Pančevo to Starčevo.

The ancient (circa 1400) monastery of **Vojlovica** [Војловица] looks rather incongruous, being surrounded on three sides by the oil refinery. It was destroyed on three occasions by Turkish invaders; most of the current structure is the result of 19th- and 20th-century reconstruction.

Continue along road (Pančevočki put) [Панчевачки пут] past football stadium L and bear R to reach centre of **Starčevo** [Старчево] (26.5km, 74m) (refreshments).

Turn L on Ive Lole Ribara [Иве Лоле Рибара] and continue on road out of village through fields. Continue on Patrijarha Arsenija Čarnojevića [Патријарха Арсенија Чарнојевића] into **Omoljica** [Омољица] (33km, 78m).

Between Omoljica and Kovin the route follows mostly unsurfaced tracks along flood dykes.

Alternative route avoiding unsurfaced tracks

Continue straight through Omoljica on Kralja Petra Prvog out of village through fields to reach **Banatski Brestovac** [Банатски Брестовац] (39.5km, 76m) (camping). Turn L at first crossroads in village on Prvomajska [Првомајска] and L again at T-junction at end of village. Follow road through fields for 5km and turn L at triangular junction to reach **Skorenovac** [Скореновац] (49km, 74m) (accommodation, refreshments). Continue straight through village on Maršala Tita [Маршала Тита] and follow road to reach outskirts of **Kovin**. Cross main road and follow Svetozara Markovica [Светозара Марковића] into town centre. Bear R beside park (Cara Lazara [Цара Лазара] and turn L at T-junction (sp Promenade Dunavac) to reach Kovin Marina (56.5km, 70m).

To continue directly on to alternative route for Stage 13 without going through town centre, turn second R after main road (1 Maj, becoming Petra Drapšina [Петра Драпшина]) passing fire station R, and continue ahead over four crossroads. At fifth crossroads, turn L (Cara Lazara) [Цара Лазара] onto the alternative route in Stage 13.

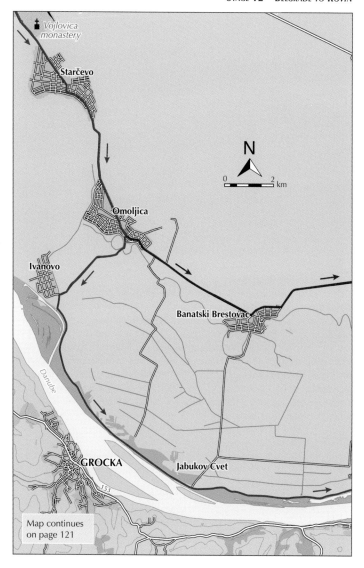

Vojlovica monastery

Starčevo

N

0 — 2 km

Omoljica

Ivanovo

Banatski Brestovac

Danube

GROCKA

153

Jabukov Cvet

Map continues on page 121

Goats on the flood dyke block the cycle track between Ivanovo and Kovin

Main route along flood dyke

Pass through village centre, where road becomes Kralja Petra Prvog [Краља Петра Првог], and 400 metres after centre, take third turn R (sp Ivanovo). Follow road over Ponjavica backwater out of village through fields towards **Ivanovo** [Иваново] (37km, 70m).

Do not enter village. Just before beginning of Ivanovo where road crosses drainage channel, turn L along flood dyke and continue to reach Danube. At first track is good quality gravel, but after a while it deteriorates into an unsurfaced track, which can become muddy when wet. Follow this track along flood dyke for 27km, passing group of weekend homes at **Jabukov Cvet** L (47.5km, 68m) (camping). Pass under pipe bridge and Smederevo road bridge then after 2km turn L off flood dyke (sp Kovin) and R onto good quality gravel track. Pass through small industrial area on asphalt road and turn R on track leading to Kovin marina. Turn L alongside marina and follow track bearing R around marina to edge of **Kovin** [Ковин] (67km, 70m) (accommodation, refreshments, tourist office, cycle shop).

Kovin (pop. 14,000) has close ties with Ráckeve in Hungary dating from the time of the Ottoman occupation when the town's Serb population fled en masse with many settling in Ráckeve. Repopulation after the Turks were expelled resulted in a mixed population of Serbs (45 per cent), Germans (20

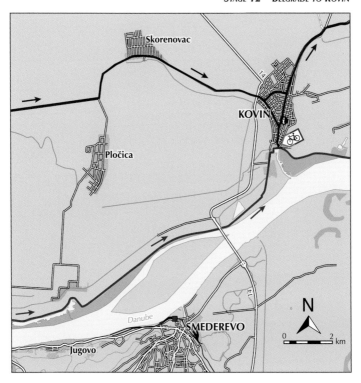

per cent), Hungarians (15 per cent) and Romanians (15 per cent). Migration, expulsion and resettlement since 1919 have seen the Serb population expand to 80 per cent today.

In Kovin the flood dyke and road routes come together briefly before going their own ways again for Stage 13, making it possible to change from one to the other.

121

STAGE 13

Kovin to Stara Palanka

Start	Kovin, marina (70m)
Finish	Stara Palanka, ferry ramp (69m)
Distance	39.5km; alternative route 40km
Waymarking	Dunavska ruta EV6

The route follows unsurfaced tracks along Danube flood dykes from Kovin to Dubovac, then a quiet road and another short section of flood dyke to the ferry port of Stara Palanka. It is flat along the flood dyke, then a slight rise and descent through woods away from the river. An alternative route uses a road from Kovin to Dubovac to avoid the unmade track along the flood dyke.

Alternative route avoiding unsurfaced tracks

From centre of **Kovin**, head north on Cara Lazara [Цара Лазара], main road out of town. After 2.5km beyond edge of town cross drainage canal and fork R (sp Gaj).

Stara Palanka beside Danube–Tisa–Danube canal

Continue on road to **Gaj** [Гај] (11.5km, 79m) (accommodation, refreshments). Cycle straight through village and continue on road to reach **Šumarak** [Шумарак] (18.5km, 99m) (accommodation). Follow road bearing R and continue to reach **Dubovac** [Дубовац)] (24km, 74m) (accommodation, refreshments, camping).

Main route along flood dyke
From **Kovin Marina** follow cycle track east along flood dyke between woods. Continue on flood dyke as it emerges beside Danube to pass R turn for riverside home development at **Manastirska Rampa** (accommodation, refreshments) (5.5km, 68m).

Continue along flood dyke passing large lagoon and more riverside homes at Raj (refreshments, camping). Continue with chimney stacks of coal mining town of Kostolac visible on opposite side of river, to reach Dubovac lagoon. Bear L through barrier onto road that serves weekend homes by lagoon and follow it turning sharply L away from lagoon. Turn R at crossroads into centre of **Dubovac** [Дубовац] (23.5km, 74m) (accommodation, refreshments, camping).

Combined route continues
Follow road through village and continue into open country ascending gently into woodland. Emerge from woods and after 1.7km cross bridge over **Danube–Tisa–Danube canal**. Immediately beyond bridge turn sharply R and L on unsurfaced track along flood dyke beside canal for 4.5km to reach ferry ramp at **Stara Palanka** [Стара Паланка] (39.5km, 69m) (accommodation, refreshments). The ferry to Ram departs every 3hrs at 0730, 1030, 1330, 1630,1930.

STAGE 14
Stara Palanka to Golubac

Start	Stara Palanka, ferry ramp (69m)
Finish	Golubac, main square (73m)
Distance	38km
Waymarking	Dunavska ruta EV6

Beyond Stara Palanka, the Danube becomes the border between Romania, north of the river and Serbia, south of it. Our route crosses by ferry to the right (south) bank and continues through Serbia passing the leisure resort of Beli Bagrem near Veliko Gradište before reaching Golubac at the entrance to the Iron Gates gorges. Apart from a steep climb away from the ferry at Ram and descent to Zatonje, the going is mostly flat and close to the river.

From **Stara Palanka**, cross Danube by ferry to **Ram** [Рам] (refreshments), with ruins of **Ottoman fortress** visible above town.

> **Ram** is a small village overlooked by the ruins of an Ottoman fortress on cliffs beside the Danube. The fortress was built in the late 15th century at a time when the Danube formed the border between the Hungarian Kingdom, north of the river, and Turkish Ottoman Empire to the south. It was constructed in the form of a regular pentagon, designed to withstand cannon warfare, with four corner towers and a gatehouse. The interior was destroyed in 1788 by advancing Austrian Habsburg forces.

From Ram ferry ramp follow road ahead uphill through village and continue into open country. Fork L after 1.5km and continue downhill to reach **Zatonje** [Затоње] (7km, 84m) (refreshments).

Just before house 59, in middle of village, turn L off main road (sp Srebrno jezero), following narrow street steeply downhill. At bottom bear L and after 100 metres turn R on road along earth dam that separates Danube from **Srebrno jezero** (Silver lake), an old Danube backwater. Continue along Danube flood dyke to reach turn-off for **Ostrovo** [Острово] (12km, 68m), which is located 500 metres south of Danube beside Srebrno jezero. Continue ahead along flood dyke

A ruined Ottoman fortress overlooks the Danube at Ram

and cycle across earth dam separating Danube and downstream end of Srebrno jezero to reach resort development of hotels and weekend homes at **Beli Bagrem** (15km, 70m) (accommodation, refreshments, camping).

Immediately over dam, turn L along track beside river and continue on asphalt cycle track past resort homes to reach beginning of Veliko Gradište. Bear L along Beogradska [Београдска] riverside promenade past boat landing stage and bear R beside park L to reach square, with town hall and Archangel Gabriel church, in centre of **Veliko Gradište** [Велико Градиште] (18.5km, 71m) (refreshments, tourist office).

Veliko Gradište (pop. 5800) was site of Pincum, a Roman settlement and castle. Nearby mines produced copper that was used to produce bronze Roman coinage, examples of which can be seen in museums in Belgrade, Berlin, London and Vienna. In medieval times the Turks built their own castle on the remains of the Roman one.

Turn R in main square on Ulica Svetosavska [Светосавска], passing church L. Where road ahead becomes one-way, turn R again (Ulica Vojvorde Mišića) [Војворде Мишића] and L (Kneza Lazara) [Кнеза Лазара]. Fork R beside gardens in middle of road and turn sharply L continuing around gardens. Bear R into Voje Bogdanovića [Воје Богдановића]. Turn half L at next junction on Albanske Spomenice [Албанске Споменице] (sp Požeženo) and follow this past large cemetery L then downhill out of town. Cross bridge over river Pec and continue through open country to reach beginning of **Požeženo** [Пожежена] (23.5km, 68m) (refreshments).

Map continues
on page 128

Turn R (do not enter village) and follow road to beginning of Vinci. Soon after entering village, turn L down narrow road to reach riverbank. This turn is easy to miss. Bear R on cycle track beside river past small marina and along riverside promenade into centre of **Vinci** [Винци] (30km, 71m) (accommodation, refreshments).

Follow cycle track through village then continue ahead beside road. Turn L at end of village onto riverside cycle track to reach **Usije** [Усије] (33km, 74m).

Where cycle track crosses ferry ramp for Romania ferry, continue ahead over small bridge and fork L onto winding cycle track. Follow this to riverbank and continue beside Danube. Emerge beside main road with first views of Iron Gates gorges and Carpathian mountains, and follow this to reach main square in centre of **Golubac** [Голубац] (38km, 73m) (accommodation, refreshments, tourist office, cycle shop).

Golubac (pop. 1650) sits at the entrance to the Đerdap (Iron Gates) gorges. The Danube at this point is 5km wide, and is used for an annual sailing regatta. Golubac castle, which stands on the riverside 4km beyond the town, is passed on the next stage.

STAGE 15
Golubac to Donji Milanovac

Start	Golubac, main square (73m)
Finish	Donji Milanovac, tourist office (72m)
Distance	57km
Waymarking	Dunavska ruta EV6

The Danube reaches a barrier formed by the Carpathian mountains and has cut the deep winding Iron Gates gorges through these mountains. This stage follows a road along the Serbian side of the gorge with steep forested slopes dropping vertically to the river. The route, mostly on an elevated position above the river, undulates gently and passes through 15 tunnels. A steep climb and descent is encountered between Boljetin and Hladne Vode. Significant historic sites are passed at Golubacki grad castle and Lepenski vir Mesolithic village.

From main square in **Golubac**, follow main road climbing gently east out of village. Road follows Danube closely to reach one of the most spectacular sights of whole journey, **Golubacki grad** [Голубачки град] ruined castle (4km, 82m).

Golubac castle has been restored to its medieval appearance

The first known reference to **Golubacki grad** castle dates from 1335 when it was described as a Hungarian fort protecting their southern border. On the front line between Hungarian and Turkish territory, it changed hands many times between Hungarians, Serbs, Ottoman Turks and Austrian Habsburgs. In 1867 it passed finally from Turkish to Serbian control and has remained Serbian (or Yugoslav) ever since. The fortress has 10 towers, up to 25m tall, with walls that stretch from the river up the steep slopes of the gorge. When the riverside road was constructed in the 1920s it passed through two huge gates cut through the walls. In 2020 a new tunnel was opened taking the road away from the castle and the old walls have been restored. The flooding of lake Đerdap (1972) caused the river to cover the lowest parts of the fortifications so the castle now appears to rise straight from the water. Castle is closed on Mondays.

Pass castle visitor centre L and follow road through tunnel by-passing ruins, then continue into hamlet of **Ridan** [Ридан] (accommodation, refreshments). Looking ahead the valley narrows rapidly with the road hugging the riverside to reach beginning of **Golubacki klisura**, the first stage of Iron Gates gorges. Once in the gorge, road is cut into riverside cliffs as it continues closely following river. Cross small bridge over river Brnjica to reach **Brnjica** [Брњица] (12km, 72m) (refreshments).

The 134km-long **Iron Gates gorges** (Serbian Đerdapska klisura; Romanian Portile de Fier) have been cut by the Danube as it forces a path through the

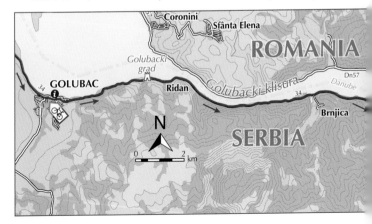

barrier formed by the Carpathian and Balkan mountains between Romania and Serbia. It is made up of four distinct gorges, where the river cuts through successive Carpathian ridges, connected by wider sections of river. Strictly speaking the name Iron Gates gorge relates only to the fourth gorge between Orsova and Sip, where the Đerdap I Dam has been constructed, but the name is widely used to describe the entire series of gorges.

The first two parts, the Golubacki klisura (Golubac gorge) between Golubac and Brnjica and the Gospodin vir (Lady's whirlpool), between Dobra and Boljetin, are traversed on this stage. The Gospodin vir has cliffs rising 500m above the river and a river depth of 82m making it the world's deepest river. The other two parts (Veliki Kazan/Mali Kazan and Iron Gate itself) are encountered during the next stage. The construction of the Đerdap I Dam has caused the river to rise by over 30m and created wide lake-like sections between the gorges, known collectively as lake Đerdap. The entire area has been incorporated into two national parks, Đerdap in Serbia and Portile de Fier in Romania.

Continue through gorge passing Čezava beach (camping) and turn-off for **Dobra** [Добра] (24km, 71m) (accommodation, refreshments) at the mouth of Dobranska valley. To reach Dobra, which is spread out along the valley R, turn L off the main road and turn back under the bridge into the village.

Main road continues following river with wooded slopes rising R. After 8km, gorge closes in tightly again as river enters **Gospodin vir** where route becomes a corniche road that winds along cliff face and passes through 15

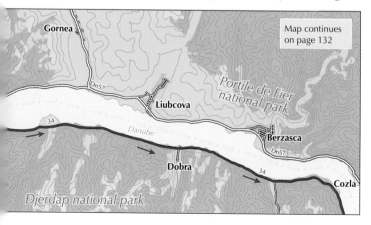

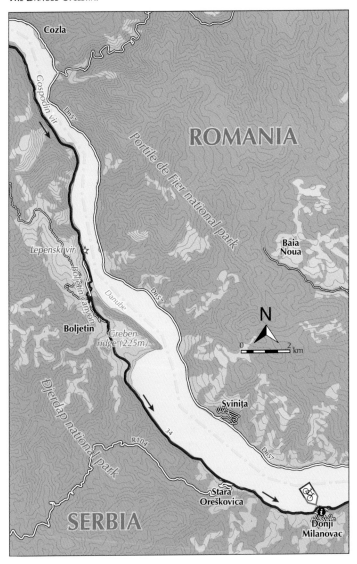

The remains of Lepenski vir mesolithic village were lifted above the Danube and covered with a protective roof

tunnels. The tunnels are unlit and some have bends inside. Make sure your lights are working. After 10km, reach turn-off L for archaeological site at **Lepenski vir** [Лепенски вир] (40km, 120m) (refreshments) and drop downhill on section of old road to main entrance.

On the riverbank at **Lepenski vir**, during work to establish the banks of the future lake Đerdap in 1965, an ancient Mesolithic village was discovered. This settlement, dating from between 7000BC and 5000BC, is one of the oldest urban sites in Europe. The inhabitants lived in tent shaped wooden houses with paved red sandstone floors, stone fireplaces and central altars. These houses were grouped in a horseshoe formation around a central square. The most significant finds were sculptures and carved figurines with fish-like features, suggesting the worship of riverine deities. The remains were moved 30m up the bank to escape being submerged beneath the lake and a large protective shelter has been built to conserve the site.

A full size plastic elephant in Donji Milanovac was a prop from the TV show Jeux sans Frontières

After visiting the Mesolithic village, continue along old road by-passing next two tunnels and descending into **Boljetin canyon** (41.5km, 89m). To avoid the drop into Boljetin canyon, you can rejoin the main road by the entrance to tunnel 6. Cross river in bottom of canyon with main road bridge soaring high above, then follow riverside road for 600m. Where road ahead leads to Boljetin village, turn sharply L uphill, then sharply R at next junction to return to main road. Road now climbs steadily for 2km away from Danube to reach a summit on **Greben ridge** (225m) with extensive views over the Danube towards Romania, then descends past small community of Hladne Vode [Хладне воде] (47km, 136m) back to riverside. Continue past turn-off for **Stara Oreškovica** [Стара Орешковица] (accommodation, refreshments, camping) to reach beginning of Donji Milanovac. Fork L parallel to Danube on Kralja Petra I [Краља Петра I] to reach tourist office in **Donji Milanovac** [Доњи милановац] (57km, 72m) (accommodation, refreshments, tourist office, cycle shop).

Donji Milanovac (pop. 2400) is a new town, built in 1970 to replace the original town, which disappeared beneath lake Đerdap after the construction of the Đerdap I Dam. St Nicholas church has wall decorations, icons and other valuable objects saved from the original village church. The riverside park has a full size plastic statue of an elephant that was originally a prop from an episode of the international TV game show *Jeux sans Frontières*.

STAGE 16
Donji Milanovac to Drobeta-Turnu Severin

Start	Donji Milanovac, tourist office (72m)
Finish	Drobeta-Turnu Severin, Tudor park (70m)
Distance	67km
Waymarking	Dunavska ruta EV6

This is the most spectacular stage of the whole journey. The route continues on a quiet main road along the Serbian side of the Iron Gates gorges with the Miroč mountains rising to the right. After passing through the dramatic Veliki Kazan, the road climbs above the Mali Kazan before descending to cross the river into Romania on a road over the Đerdap I Dam. The stage ends by following a busy road into Drobeta-Turnu Severin.

From tourist office in **Donji Milanovac** follow cycle route east, at first along pedestrianised part of Kralja Petra I, passing an elephant statue in park L, then continuing on road beside Danube to reach main road. Follow this out of town and continue round headland at point where river Porečka joins Danube. Bear R, following Porečka away from Danube for 2.4km then cross this river and turn L at T-junction (4.5km, 81m) on opposite bank. Follow Porečka back to Danube and continue along riverbank past **Golubinje** [Голубиње] (11km, 85m), a village that climbs up the gorge side R.

Cycle past tiny hamlet of Malo Golubinje (accommodation), continuing to hug riverside, then ascend steadily to reach longest tunnel (T4, 371 metres long). Descend towards river through two short tunnels passing **Veliki Kazan** gorge (Great Cauldron), third and most spectacular part of Iron Gates. The gorge here is at its narrowest (150 metres) with the Danube powering through the gap. After a brief widening, with Dubova at back of lagoon on Romanian side of river, gorge narrows again to **Mali Kazan** gorge (Little Cauldron). Route now starts ascending steeply through final tunnel with view of **Mraconia monastery**, which sits beside Danube far below on Romanian side of gorge. As road continues ascending, there is a view of **Decebalus Rex** monument, carved into the cliffside opposite.

The 40m high Decebalus Rex monument is carved into the rock face of the gorge

Monumental **Decebalus Rex**, the tallest rock sculpture in Europe, is a huge figure hewn from the cliffside on the Romanian side of the gorge by the mouth of the river Mraconia. Paid for by a Romanian industrialist at a cost of over one million euros, it took 12 sculptors 10 years (1994–2004) to complete the 40m-high statue. The sculpture portrays the head of Decebalus (which translates as 'strong as ten men'), the last king of Dacia who reigned from AD87 until being defeated by the Romans in AD106.

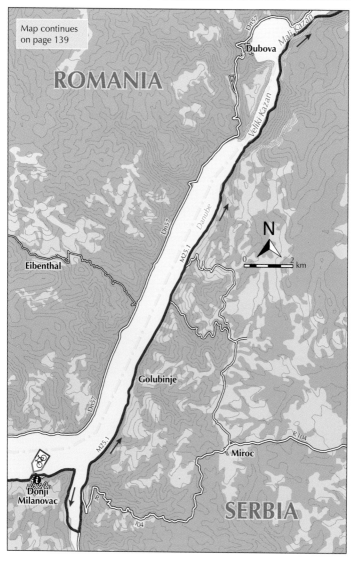

Map continues
on page 139

ROMANIA

Eibenthal

Dubova

Mali Kazan

Veliki Kazan

Dn57

M25.1

Danube

N

0   2 km

Golubinje

Dn57

M25.1

R 104

Miroc

Donji
Milanovac

R

104

SERBIA

After 4km of steady ascent, summit is reached at **Golo Brdo** [Голо Брдо] (32.5km, 276m).

The **Tabula Traiana**, below Golo Brdo and visible only from the river, is a four-metre by two-metre memorial plaque carved into the cliffside. This commemorates the completion in AD100 of a Roman road through the Iron Gates gorges commissioned by the Emperor Trajan. This road, a major engineering achievement that was hewn from the rock face, served Roman military settlements along the Danube. It was an enabling factor in the Romans' successful invasion of Dacia in AD105. When the Đerdap I Dam was being built (1972) the plaque was cut from the rock and moved 40m higher up the cliff face so as to remain above river level. The road was not so lucky and it disappeared beneath the water.

River widens again as road descends to riverbank and continues to **Tekija** [Текија] (40km, 76m) (accommodation, refreshments, camping).

Below Tekija, there is view of Orşova, once an important port, now a Romanian new town that spreads around a large lagoon created by the Đerdap

Mali Kazan (Little Cauldron), part of Iron Gates gorges

Map continues on page 140

I Dam. The road bears R passing an innocuous pile of bricks that were once part of **Fort Elizabeth**, an Austrian fort built in 1736 to control navigation on the river. Continue following river to reach road junction near **Novi Sip** (53km, 80m) (accommodation, refreshments). Turn L (sp Drobeta) and follow road zigzagging to **Serbian border post** before **Iron Gates I Dam**. The Romanians are very security sensitive regarding the dam and photography is prohibited, the rules being strictly enforced by armed guards on every corner.

Đerdap (Iron Gates) I Dam was the first of two dams built across the Đerdap gorge. An agreement to construct these huge hydro-electric dams had been signed, in 1964, by the Romanian and Yugoslav governments. The first was located near Sip, and was completed in 1972. When it was built it was one of the largest hydro-electric power stations in the world producing over 2000MW of electricity.

When the dam was completed, the water level behind the dam rose by 35m resulting in 17,000 residents of towns and villages in the gorge needing to be relocated to higher ground. The most famous victim of the rise in water level was the island of Ada Kaleh, which was 3km downstream from Orşova.

139

This island had a mainly Turkish population, a throwback to the days when the whole region was under Ottoman control. Most of the residents emigrated to Turkey when the island was flooded.

In addition to producing electricity, the dam greatly improved navigation. Two huge locks raise 5000-tonne vessels by 34m up to lake Đerdap where calmer water has replaced the strong flow previously encountered by boats transiting the gorge.

Cross Danube on road over dam, passing an EV6 sign with the message: *Good bye. You are leaving Serbia. 'Don't cry because it's over – smile because it happened. We wish your bike to always have tires full of air, and chain always ready to transfer your dreams to roads and paths. Have a nice rolling in beautiful Romania'.*

On Romanian side of river turn L through **border post** and R onto busy main road where cycling is possible on, albeit narrow, hard shoulder. Continue past electricity sub-station R and pass **Gura Văii** (56.5km, 74m) (station).

Continue close to Danube and pass roadside restaurant and service area at Sârbului R (refreshments). Continue ahead at roundabout (do not follow Drobeta-Turnu Severin by-pass which bears L) and continue on Calea Timişoarei through **Schela Cladovei** (63.5km, 74m) (accommodation, refreshments).

Cycle past shipyards and industrial area to reach roundabout with representation of Trajan's Roman bridge in centre. Continue ahead (Bvd Carol 1) passing station R. Join cycle track R and continue past Rozelor park, Eroilor Heroes' monument and Hotel Continental (all R) to reach **Tudor park** L and **Palace of culture** R in centre of **Drobeta-Turnu Severin** (67km, 70m) (accommodation, refreshments, cycle shop, station).

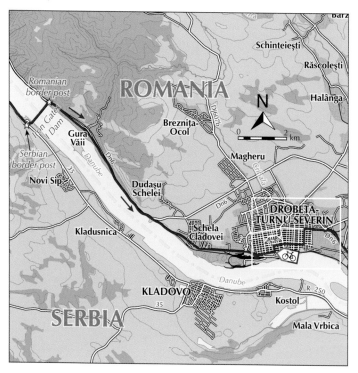

DROBETA-TURNU SEVERIN

Drobeta-Turnu Severin (pop. 80,000) was the site of one of the great wonders of the Roman world. In AD103 the Roman Emperor Trajan commissioned a bridge over the Danube as a precursor to his planned invasion of Dacia. Known as Trajan's bridge, it was designed by Apollodorus of Damascus, the leading architect of the time, and was completed in only three years. Twenty masonry pillars supported wooden oak arches, which carried a 15-metre-wide and 1km-long platform, raised 19m above the river. There were stone castra (small castles) guarding the entrances on each bank. When the Romans withdrew from Dacia in AD270, the bridge was destroyed to prevent barbarian attacks across the river. Before completion of Portile de Fier II Dam (1984), a number of ruined pillars could still be seen at times of low water, but nowadays only two are visible.

Drobeta was founded as a Roman settlement on the Dacian side of the bridge. It grew rapidly and by the third century had a population of

40,000 and all the accoutrements of Roman civilisation (forum, bath houses, temples, basilica and theatre). The Byzantine successors to the Romans built a tower called Turnu Severin (Tower of Severus) near the remains of Trajan's Bridge and the city's modern name (used since 1972) reflects these two antecedents. In the 11th century the Hungarians built Severin fortress using material from the Roman castrum. This changed hands many times between Hungarians, Romanians and Ottoman Turks. When the Turks finally left in 1829, the Romanians began to develop the town with road and rail

The Castelul de Apu water tower is the symbol of Drobeta-Turnu Severin

connections, shipyards and municipal buildings. The Castelul de Apa water tower, nowadays the emblem of the city, was built in 1914. In the inter-war and communist periods development continued with buildings including the Palace of culture and attractive parks, gardens and fountains. Away from the centre, high density Soviet style housing surrounded the city. Since the fall of communism (1989), the economy has stagnated, with the city's isolation restricting the amount of industrial investment and the population has fallen from 115,000 (1992) to 80,000 (2021).

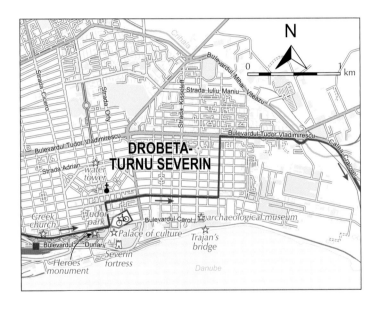

STAGE 17

Drobeta-Turnu Severin to Gruia

Start	Drobeta-Turnu Severin, Tudor park (70m)
Finish	Gruia church (94m)
Distance	71.5km
Waymarking	None, follow first Dn6, then Dn56a, Dn56b and finally Dn56c

This is a long stage that first follows a cycle track through Drobeta before leaving the city on a busy main road. The route soon turns onto quiet country roads that undulate through a succession of villages away from the Danube. There are long stretches through open country with little or no shade. Most villages have a shop selling provisions, but there is no accommodation after Hinova until Gruia.

From **Tudor park** in Drobeta-Turnu Severin cycle north (Str Theodor Costescu) between park L and Cinetică fountain R. Str Theodor Costescu is a pedestrian street with dedicated cycle lane L. Where pedestrianisation ends, turn R (Calea Traian) using cycle track R. Go ahead over nine crossroads and where cycle track ends turn L beside house 275 (Str Anghel Saligny) using cycle lane R.

Where this reaches dual carriageway main road (Bvd Tudor Vladimirescu), turn R on cycle track R beside road. Go ahead at roundabout (second exit) where cycle track ends, then continue into Str Craiovei, downhill through an industrial area and into open country. Go ahead at next roundabout (where by-pass re-joins) onto Dn6, a busy main road where

Many people in Romania still obtain water from wells like this one in Batoţi

Map continues
on page 147

Early morning fishermen at Ostrovul Corbului

cycling is possible on hard shoulder. Go over river Topolniţa and cross two railway bridges (one under, one over). Pass through edge of **Şimian** (7km, 59m) (accommodation, refreshments).

Fork R at road junction (Dn56a, another busy road) and continue through open country parallel with Danube to reach **Hinova** (16.5km, 45m) (accommodation, refreshments).

Turn R at road junction onto quiet country road (Dn56b). Cross old course of Danube and continue along riverside through **Ostrovul Corbului** to reach lower part of **Batoţi** (24.5km, 49m).

Bear L away from river uphill into higher part of village, then fork L (sp Portile de Fier II) and continue steadily uphill through open country and woodland. After passing summit (146m) descend to edge of **Devesel** (30km, 110m), which also goes by name of Chilia.

Turn R at T-junction and L after 600 metres, continuing out of village across an agricultural plateau and continue on asphalt road to **Burila Mare** (38km, 102m).

Follow asphalt road bearing R and L through village, then continue on plateau before descending through woodland to reach edge of **Tigănaşi** (44.5km, 83m).

Bear L at T-junction and continue on road parallel with, and descending towards, Danube. Pass turn-off R leading to Portile de Fier II Dam, then climb gently away from river to **Gogoşu** (54.5km, 77m).

Map continues
on page 148

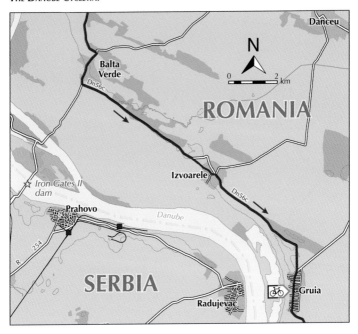

Bear R following road (now Dn56c) winding through village, then descend round series of bends into **Balta Verde** (58km, 49m).

Follow asphalt road turning L at end of village and continue level and straight through woods. Where road bears L and starts ascending, fork R on gravel track which after 500m becomes asphalt. Fork L ahead into **Izvoarele** (65.5km, 73m).

Follow road over three crossroads, then at fourth turn R to rejoin main road. Continue on river terrace with extensive views in all directions, then bear R at T-junction to reach **Gruia** (71.5km, 94m) (accommodation, refreshments, reservation essential). To find the hotel/restaurant, turn R opposite the church (no sp) and follow the road winding downhill for 1.75km to Portul Gruia on the Danube riverbank.

STAGE 18
Gruia to Calafat

Start	Gruia, church (94m)
Finish	Calafat, town hall (54m)
Distance	62.5km
Waymarking	None, follow Dn56c, then Dn56a and finally Dn56

The route continues on a quiet country road that runs along the crest of the river terrace, with the Danube visible across the flood plain R. At about the half way point, traffic becomes heavier as main roads are followed into Calafat. The only intermediate accommodation is near Cetate.

Map continues on page 150

From centre of **Gruia**, follow Dn56c south through village and open fields, then fork R to reach **Pristol** (5.5km, 52m). Continue across plateau, then turn steeply uphill round zigzag bend into **Gîrla Mare** (11.5km, 82m).

Continue through fields and go straight ahead through **Vrata** (17.5km, 60m), continuing on river terrace before descending onto flood plain to reach **Salcia** (26.5km, 41m).

Fork L in village and continue through fields for 4.5km to T-junction. Turn R onto Dn56a (main road with cycling possible on hard shoulder), and follow this steeply uphill into **Cetate** (37.5km, 85m) (accommodation, refreshments at Port Cetate).

On the banks of the Danube below Cetate is **Culture Port Cetate**. Here are the warehouses and quays of an old grain port that from 1880 until 1945 exported wheat from south-eastern Romania to Austria. Closed in 1945, when the flow of wheat changed to head by rail towards Moscow and not by boat to Vienna, the buildings fell into disrepair. In 1997 the Romanian poet Mircea Dinescu purchased the derelict site and has overseen its conversion into this thriving multi-art community which hosts artistic events and festivals. Rooms

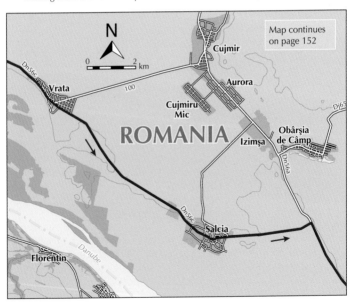

are available for overnight stays and the restaurant specialises in innovative cooking using local produce and wine.

After village, follow main road as it passes **Moreni** R and continues to **Hunia** (45.5km, 80m) and **Maglavit** (47.5km, 75m) (station).

In early 1930s **Petre Lupu**, an illiterate shepherd, had a vision of God in the forest west of Maglavit. Pilgrims drawn to the spot claimed miraculous events had occurred and, in 1935, construction of a monastery and church began. Work ceased during the communist period (1946–1989) when the area was cleared as a security zone due to its proximity to the national border. Building recommenced in 1989, but sadly Lupu (who had been imprisoned by the communists) died in 1994 before its completion in 2006. His body was reburied at the monastery in 2009.

The grave of Petre Lupu, a shepherd whose visions inspired the building of the Maglavit monastery

Continue for 1km to reach T-junction (refreshments) and turn R (Dn56). Follow this road straight ahead through **Golenți** (52.5km, 68m) (refreshments, station) and **Basarabi** (56.5km, 63m) (accommodation, refreshments) to reach major road junction. Keep R then continue ahead over approach road to bridge linking Calafat with Vidin in Bulgaria, which can be seen R. It is possible to cycle on the pavement by joining it where it starts soon after the road junction. Go straight ahead at roundabout (Str Traian) and cycle downhill to reach crossroads with pedestrianised Bvd Tudor Vladimirescu, which is part way down the hill. Turn L along this street to reach town hall R in centre of **Calafat** (62.5km, 54m) (accommodation, refreshments, cycle shop, station).

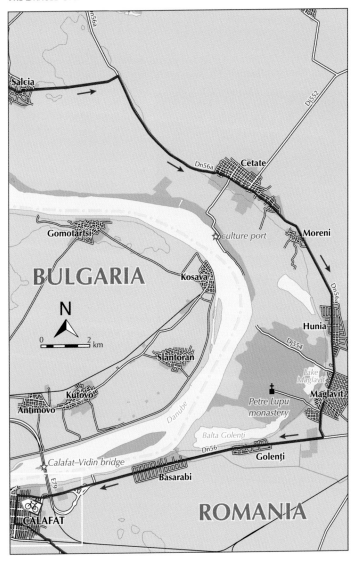

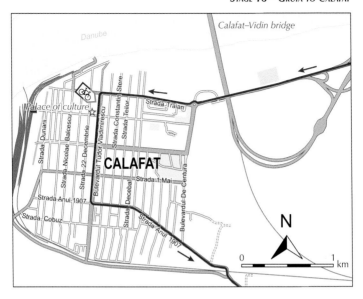

The small riverside town of **Calafat** (pop. 13,750) was established in the 14th century by Genoese colonists who set up ship repairing facilities beside the river. For many years it was a frontier trading town between Romanians, Hungarians and Serbs to the north and Ottoman Turks to the south, before becoming part of the Ottoman Empire. In 1854, during the Crimean War, when Calafat was a Turkish army stronghold, Russian forces heading up the Danube besieged the town for four months but were unable to capture it. Plans to build a bridge across the Danube to Vidin (Bulgaria), first mooted in 1925, were realised in 2013 when a 2km-long combined four-lane road, rail and cycleway bridge opened.

STAGE 19
Calafat to Bechet

Start	Calafat, town hall (54m)
Finish	Bechet, Dn55 junction (40m)
Distance	96km
Waymarking	None, follow Dn55a

This is the first of several stages that follow the Romanian Danube road through a sandy landscape along the edge of a river terrace, about 30m above the flood plain. The environment is one of seemingly endless intensive agriculture producing grain, sunflowers, grapes and other produce. A series of villages and small towns are passed, but there is not much in the way of tourist infrastructure and no accommodation until near Bechet. The road has little traffic and is generally level with a few gentle inclines.

From pedestrian precinct in centre of **Calafat**, follow Bvd Tudor Vladimirescu south, becoming dual carriageway road after first junction. Pass courthouse L and continue ahead over roundabout going gently uphill. At next roundabout at top of hill, turn L (Str 1907, Dn55a) and follow this road as it bears R out of town. Cross railway level crossing and fork L, then continue gently down-hill straight ahead through fields to reach town of **Poiana Mare** (14.5km, 39m) (refreshments).

In a park in the centre of **Poiana Mare** (pop. 9000) is a small pavilion built in 1830 by Prince Milos Obrenovic of Serbia, which hosted a convention (1835) that agreed an economic treaty between Romania and Serbia (at that time semi-autonomous vassal states of Ottoman Turkey). Later meetings in the same building drew up a secret treaty against the Turks and for a short period during the Romanian Liberation war (1877) it was headquarters for the Romanian army. A plaque recalling these events was removed in 1949 by the communist government, who supressed teaching this period of Romanian history. It was restored in 1992 after the fall of communism.

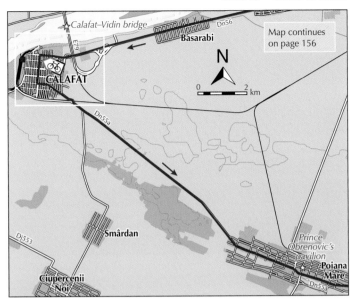

Map continues on page 156

For a short period in 1877 this pavilion in Poiana Mare was the headquarters of the Romanian army

Horse-drawn cart and sunflowers, two common sights in Romanian agriculture

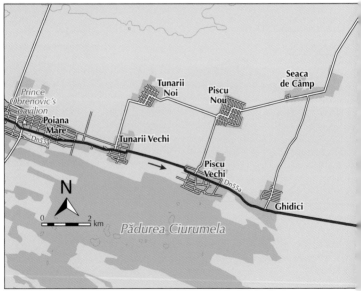

Pass park in town centre and continue through town into adjoining community of **Tunarii Vechi** (18.5km, 40m). Follow main road as it zigzags L and R out of village, then continues between fields and zigzags R and L into **Piscu Vechi** (22.5km, 37m). Follow road through **Ghidici** (25km, 35m).

Main road continues straight and level between fields into **Rast** (32.5km, 32m) and continues to reach **Negoi** (40km, 40m).

Continue through fields into **Catane** (45km, 39m) and follow road bearing R in village then through fields. Pass through **Bistreţu Nou** (51km, 36m) to reach **Bistreţ** (54km, 34m). Pass ruins of old church L just before centre of village, then continue out of village bearing R to cycle alongside **lake Bistreţul** R, second largest lake in Romania.

Continue through **Plosca** (56km, 33m) and cross bridge over river Desnăţui into **Cârna** (62km, 32m). Go through village then pass end of lake Bistreţul and follow road through **Săpata** (68km, 32m).

At next village, **Măceşu de Jos** (71.5km, 34m), bear R at beginning of village then turn R at crossroads and first L to continue with low lying wetland of Danube flood plain R. Climb gently through edge of **Nedeia** (77km, 46m) and descend into **Gighera** (79.5km, 38m).

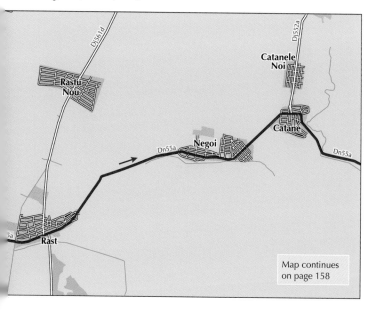

Map continues on page 158

Ruins of an old church in Bistreţ

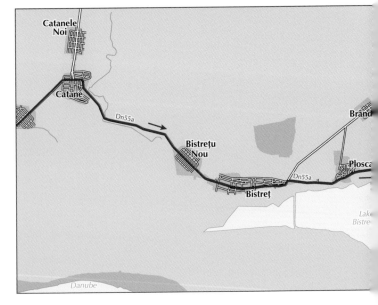

Continue beside Danube flood plain then ascend to river terrace to reach **Zǎval** (83km, 47m) and turn R in middle of village. Descend to cross bridge over river Jiu, passing campsite R (basic accommodation, refreshments, camping), and cycle through **Pǎdurea Zǎval** state forest. Cross river Jiet bridge and turn R into **Ostroveni** (90km, 42m).

Pass through village, with church and outdoor theatre L, and continue on straight tree-lined road. At T-junction with Dn55 main road, turn R (Str Alexandru Ioan Cuza) into **Bechet** (96km, 40m) (accommodation, refreshments). Stage ends by road junction where Dn55 leads R to Bechet ferry.

Simple church belfry in Ostroveni

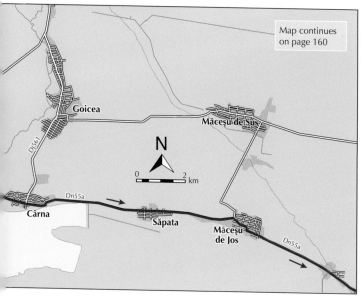

Map continues on page 160

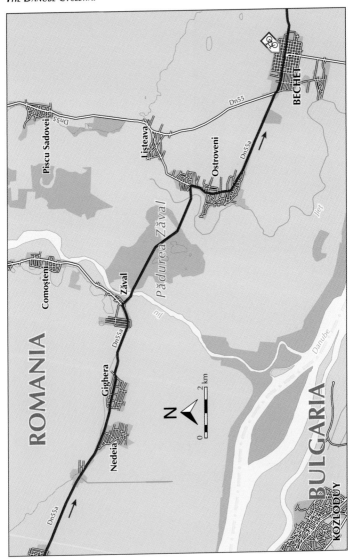

STAGE 20
Bechet to Corabia

Start	Bechet, Dn55 junction (40m)
Finish	Corabia, post office (47m)
Distance	45.5km
Waymarking	none, follow Dn54a

This stage continues to follow the Danube road along the river terrace through a sandy landscape particularly suited to growing melons. A series of small towns and villages is passed with little of interest until Corabia. The road, which is generally level with a few gentle climbs onto and off the river terrace, is busier than the previous stage.

In middle of **Bechet**, where Dn55 turns R towards ferry for Bulgaria, keep ahead (Str Alexandru Ioan Cuza, Dn54a) and continue out of village through fields, then ascend gently through **Călăraşi** (7km, 53m).

Cycle through village and continue on Str Victoriei into **Dăbuleni** (11.5km, 57m). The town is known for the production of melons; north of the town is an

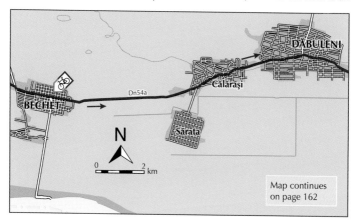

Map continues on page 162

area of sandy soil and dunes known as the Oltenian Sahara. Continue out of town on Str Unirii descending into open country. Pass turn-off L for **Ianca** and follow road ascending again through **Potelu** (20,5km, 53m).

Road continues through **Grojdibodu** (26.5km, 49m), **Gura Padinii** (30.5km, 39m), **Orlea Nouă** and bears L to pass **Orlea** (35km, 43m). Road continues straight ahead through fields, becoming Str Celeiului as it reaches **Cartier Celei** (41.5km, 40m).

> The ruins of **Cetatii Sucidava** Roman castle, on the southern edge of Cartier Celei, overlook the Danube flood plain. Built in AD275, towards the end of Roman occupation of Dacia, it remained in Byzantine hands until destruction by invading Huns in AD600. Within the ruins the most interesting discovery was the *fântână secretă* (secret well), an 18-metre lined shaft to an underground spring connected to the fortress by a 26-metre-long underground corridor intended to provide access to water during times of siege. Legend says that water from the well intensifies romance and wedding couples used to visit the spring to guarantee eternal love. Other ruins include Roman baths, paved streets, rooms with hypocaust underfloor heating and an early Christian basilica. Unfortunately the site is in poor repair and no longer open to the public.
>
> In AD328 the Roman Emperor Constantine the Great commissioned a bridge over the Danube at Sucidava. At a length of 2.5km, it was the longest bridge constructed by the Romans. It survived less than 40 years; the reason for its demise is unknown.

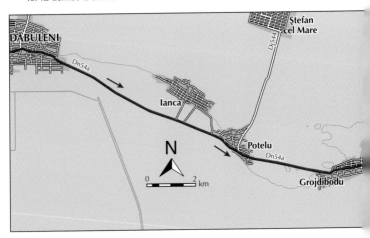

Hypocaust underfloor heating at Cetatii Sucidava Roman castle near Cartier Celei

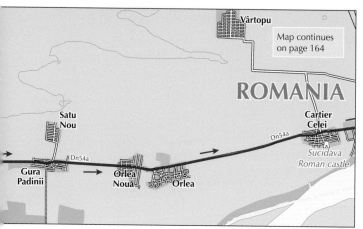

Map continues on page 164

163

Continue out of village on Str Traian, passing ruined Soviet era industrial area. Pass road L leading to Corabia by-pass and go ahead over railway crossing into Str Carpați. Soon after grim Soviet era housing blocks L, reach end of stage at post office L by entrance to Piața Eroilor (Heroes Square) in **Corabia** (45.5km, 47m) (accommodation, refreshments, cycle shop, station). Turn L beside the post office to reach the centre of town.

Corabia (pop. 13,500) translates into English as 'ship' – appropriately so as the town was created in the late 19th century around a new port on the Danube. Local grain merchants first mooted the idea of developing the area in 1859, wishing to reduce obstacles to trade imposed by landowners. Approved by the Romanian parliament in 1871, work finally started in 1880. Steady growth, particularly industrial development during the communist area, led to a population of 22,500 by 1992. Subsequently this has declined as inefficient communist era factories have closed and people have moved away to seek employment. The main places of interest, town hall, cathedral and Heroes monument, are grouped together in Piața Eroilor.

STAGE 21
Corabia to Turnu Măgurele

Start	Corabia, post office (47m)
Finish	Turnu Măgurele, central park (36m)
Distance	30.5km
Waymarking	None, follow Dn54

This short stage continues to follow the Danube road, at first along the river terrace, then dropping down onto the flood plain to cross the river Olt and back up onto the terrace to end in Turnu Măgurele. The countryside is more open than it was on the previous stage, with few villages en route.

From post office in centre of **Corabia**, cycle east along main road (Str Carpaţi, becoming Str Dumitru Buzdun, Dn54) out of town into **Cartier Siliştioara**. Two large monuments to events in Romanian Independence war of 1877 are passed, **military monument** L and illuminated heroes cross R. Continue on Str Dunării into open country, with Danube below cliffs R and straight ahead to reach **Gîrcov** (9km, 36m).

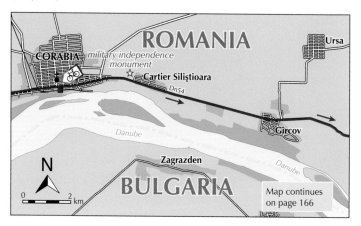

Map continues on page 166

Continue through village on main road (Str Principală) then through fields to edge of **Islaz** (20.5km, 31m) (accommodation, refreshments).

Islaz (pop. 4250) became famous in June 1848 (known throughout Europe as the year of Revolutions) when revolutionaries in Romania issued the Proclamation of Islaz. This listed 22 objectives of the Wallachian Revolution including independence from foreign domination, emancipation of peasants, regular elections and equal rights regardless of race or religion. The revolutionaries marched north from Islaz, becoming 150,000 strong by the time they reached Craiova. Despite initial success with the fall of the government in Bucharest, internal disagreements between the revolutionaries, particularly over land reform, and military intervention by Ottoman and Russian troops ended the revolution in late September. Although the seeds of change had been set, it took 70 years for all of the demands to be achieved.

Follow road ahead through fields to cross bridge over river Olt then continue across flood plain and cross second bridge over smaller river Sâi. The Olt is a major river that rises in the Carpathians and drains much of southern Wallachia. Climb gently on Str Popa Şapcă into Turnu Măgurele. Stage ends at central park in **Turnu Măgurele** (30.5km, 36m) (accommodation, refreshments, cycle shop).

Turnu Măgurele (pop. 19,500), which translates as 'hill tower', sits on the edge of the river terrace overlooking the Danube flood plain. Originally fortified by the Byzantine Emperor Justinian in the sixth century it was captured by the

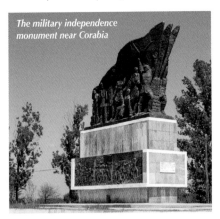
The military independence monument near Corabia

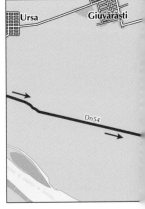

Ottoman Turks in 1417 and remained Turkish until 1829. During the Romanian Independence War (1877–1878) the city was the base for Romanian military activity across the Danube in Bulgaria, commemorated by a monument in central park. Also in central park are the local theatre and St Haralambos Orthodox cathedral, which was built 1900–1902 in combined baroque and Byzantine style. During an earthquake on 4 March 1977, the main tower collapsed and was subsequently rebuilt. Industrial development during communist times saw the building of a textile plant and a large chemical works beside the river, notorious for high levels of pollution. The population peaked at 37,000 in 1992, before falling as residents left to find employment elsewhere.

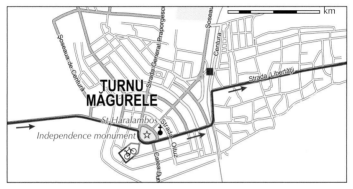

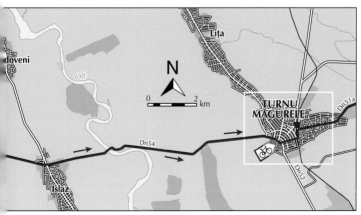

STAGE 22
Turnu Măgurele to Zimnicea

Start	Turnu Măgurele, central park (36m)
Finish	Zimnicea, town hall (34m)
Distance	57km
Waymarking	None, follow Dn51a

The route continues to follow the Danube road, at first along the side of the flood plain. After crossing the river Călmățui, the road climbs onto the river terrace above lake Suhaia bird reserve before descending to Zimnicea.

From Str Republicii, the one-way system around central park in **Turnu Măgurele**, cycle east on Str Vlad Țepeș (Dn51a). Cross railway line and turn immediately L (Str Ion Creangă). Bear R (Str Libertății) and continue out of town and through open country to **Ciuperceni** (6.5km, 28m).

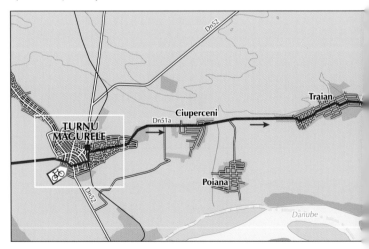

Follow road through fields to reach **Traian** (12km, 35m) (refreshments) and through more fields to **Seaca** (16.5km, 33m). Seaca has many very large and ornate partly built houses spread throughout the village. These have been constructed by Roma families as an ostentatious way of demonstrating their wealth. Continue without a break in built-up area, rising gently at first then undulating through **Năvodari** (20km, 49m).

Unfinished house in Seaca

Continue through fields to **Vânători** (25.5km, 28m) and on to **Lisa** (30.5km, 30m). Immediately after the village, cross river Călmățui and start ascending ridge on opposite side of bridge. At T-Junction on edge of **Piatra**, turn R away from village and continue ascending into **Viişoara** (35km, 70m).

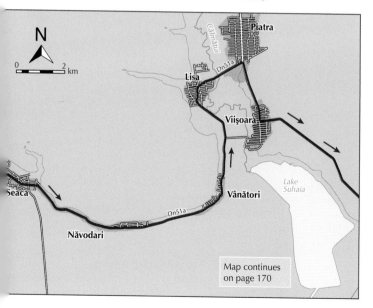

Map continues on page 170

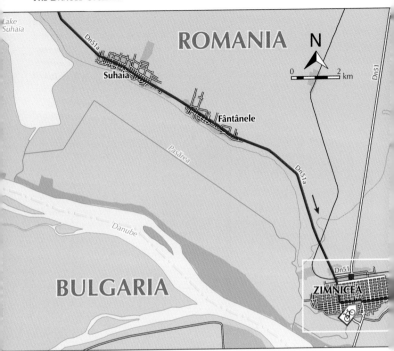

Bear L (Str Şuseaua Mare-D) at road junction in centre of village, continuing to ascend for 500m to reach summit (92m), then cross irrigation canal and follow road through fields along ridge top to reach **Suhaia** (43.5km, 79m).

Suhaia (pop. 1900) sits on the edge of the river terrace above lake Suhaia, a bird reserve with similar ecological conditions to the Danube Delta, although the lake cannot be seen from the road. Both lake and village were originally under the patronage of Cotlomuz monastery on Mt Athos in northern Greece.

Continue along crest of ridge above very fertile irrigated agricultural land that was once part of lake Suhaia into the village of **Fântânele** (pop. 1300) (46.5km, 83m). Fântânele, which translates as 'springs', was originally situated below the ridge along the spring line beside the lake, but was moved up on to the ridge in 1930. Follow road along ridge with distant views of Bulgarian hills across Danube flood plain R, then descend steadily through fields and cross railway level crossing. At junction with Dn51 main road go straight ahead (Str Turnu Măgurele) over another level crossing. Cross series of minor crossroads, taking eighth turn L (Str Ştefan cel Mare) (sp Centru). Follow this past **central park** to reach **town hall** R in centre of **Zimnicea** (57km, 34m) (accommodation, refreshments, cycle shop).

Zimnicea (pop.12,500), the most southerly town in Romania, has a few scant remains of a Dacian fortress from the fourth century BC which is said to have been used to defend the area from attacks by Lysimachos, Macedonian governor of Dacia under Alexander the Great. The town suffered badly during the 1977 Romanian earthquake. A lot of buildings were destroyed and many of those that survived were subsequently demolished to make way for a communist era planned new town. Unfortunately building standards were low and much of the newly built infrastructure has been affected by poor workmanship. Under communism, industrial development brought a number of factories to Zimnicea and boosted the population to 17,000. Since 1989, many of these have closed and the population has fallen below 13,000.

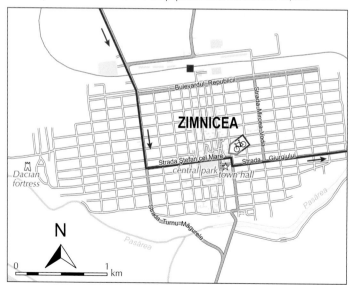

STAGE 23

Zimnicea to Giurgiu

Start	Zimnicea, town hall (34m)
Finish	Giurgiu, Turkish watchtower (24m)
Distance	60km
Waymarking	None, follow Dn5c

This stage continues to follow the Danube road mostly along the flood plain between the river terrace and the Pasărea backwater of the Danube. The route passes through a series of large villages strung out along the road. Apart from one short climb onto the river terrace, this stage is level.

From front of town hall in centre of **Zimnicea**, follow Str Ştefan cel Mare east and turn immediately R (Str Primăverii) and first L (Str Giurgiului). Follow this road (Dn5c) out of town over railway level crossing and continue to **Zimnicele** (4.5km, 28m).

Follow road through village to reach **Năsturelu** (8.5km, 26m). Continue beside river terrace, which rises as sandy cliffs L, cross bridge over river Vedea and turn R at T-junction into **Bujoru** (18km, 26m).

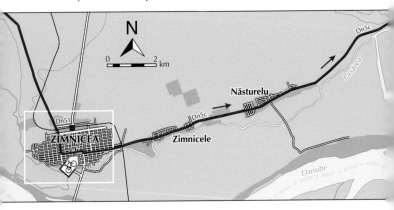

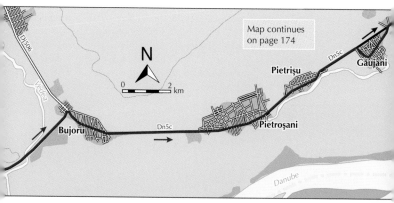

Map continues on page 174

Roma cart near Bujoru

As part of a 1930s irrigation and flood prevention scheme, the river **Vedea** was canalised and a direct outlet to the Danube opened south of Bujoru. An old course of the Danube known as the river Pasărea, which flows parallel to the main river before joining it below Giurgiu, was incorporated in the scheme. Parts of the Pasărea can be seen occasionally to the right of the road along this stage.

After village, road climbs onto river terrace (summit 50m), then descends again to reach **Pietroşani** (24.5km, 25m). There are only a couple of fields to pass before reaching next village of **Pietrişu** (28km, 25m). Continue to reach road junction at beginning of **Găujani** (31.5km, 28m). For a 500-metre shorter but rougher route, continue straight ahead, through the edge of Găujani, on a poorly surfaced road that re-joins the main road at the end of the village.

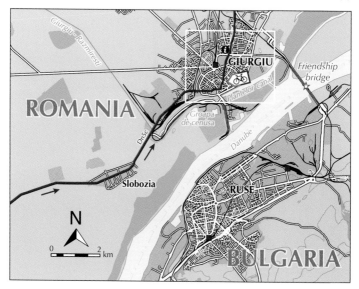

Follow asphalt road bearing R then curving L through village centre. After Găujani, continue through fields into **Cetăţuia** (35km, 25m) and on to **Vedea** (39km, 27m). In middle of village, follow asphalt road turning L at offset cross-roads. Vedea is a long drawn out village, with only a short gap before next village of **Malu** (44km, 26m). After leaving Malu, Bulgarian city of Ruse [Pyce] can be seen R on hillside on opposite side of Danube.

After village of **Slobozia** (53.5km, 29m), more fields, now with view of industrial dereliction ahead heralding the beginning of Giurgiu, which is entered over a railway bridge leading to Sos Sloboziei passing derelict factories L. Follow road under second railway bridge into Bvd 1907 passing some very run-down Soviet era housing blocks R. At five-way road junction turn L (not sharp L) into Mircea cel Bărtrân (cycle lane R) and follow this to reach Piaţa Unirii square in centre of **Giurgiu** (60km, 24m) with old **Turkish watchtower** in middle (accommodation, refreshments, tourist office, cycle shop, station). Although the stage ends in the city centre, it may be preferable to continue on to Stage 24, through the city, to the northern suburbs where accommodation can be found.

175

The Friendship bridge connects Giurgiu with Ruse in Bulgaria

Giurgiu (pop. 55,000) was founded in the 14th century by a group of Genoese merchants who named it after San Giorgio, the patron saint of Genoa. The town was under Turkish Ottoman occupation for over 400 years (1420–1829) as a major point to control traffic on the Danube. After near destruction during the Russo-Turkish wars it was rebuilt as a planned city to a radial plan around a central market. Heavily bombed during the Second World War when it was a transhipping point for Romanian oil destined for Germany, it was rebuilt again post-war by the communists as an industrial city and inland port. The 2.8km-long combined road/rail double-deck Friendship bridge, the first bridge built across the Danube between Romania and Bulgaria since Roman times, was opened in 1954 between Giurgiu and Ruse [Pyce] in Bulgaria. Much of the industrial development that took place during the communist period has closed with the city's population declining from 74,000 (1992) to 55,000 (2021). The main tourist sights include the ruins of Cetatea Giurgiului 14th-century fortress, Turnul Ceasornicului Turkish watchtower, St Nicholas Church (1830) commissioned by Tsar Nicholas I to commemorate Russian victory over Turkey in 1829 and Bizetz bridge over a canal, which claims to be the world's first curved girder bridge.

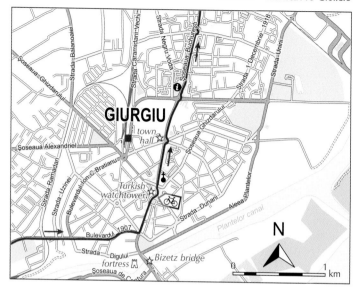

The Bizetz bridge in Giurgiu claims to be the world's first curved girder bridge

STAGE 24
Giurgiu to Olteniţa

Start	Giurgiu, Turkish watchtower (24m)
Finish	Olteniţa, central park (18m)
Distance	76km
Waymarking	None, follow Dn5 then Dn41

The stage starts by following a busy highway out of Giurgiu, then branches off along the Danube road climbing onto the river terrace. The well-surfaced road passes through a number of prosperous villages before dropping down to the flood plain to cross the river Argeş and finish at Olteniţa.

From Piaţa Unirii by **Turkish watchtower** in centre of Giurgiu, follow Sos Bucureşti north. Go ahead at first roundabout passing town hall L. Continue past modern hospital with stepped roof R and go ahead over second roundabout. Pass statue of Mihai Viteazu in park L, then modern fountain in front of curved apartment blocks. Continue following Sos Bucureşti out of city under railway bridge and past Kaufland shopping centre L. Go ahead at roundabout where road from Bulgaria via Friendship bridge joins from R. Pass through industrial area of Giurgiu Nord (accommodation, refreshments, station) where there is attractive little **St Gheorghe monastery** surrounded by industrial buildings L, into **Remuş** (6km, 23m).

Continue on busy dual carriageway road (Dn5) with cycling possible on hard shoulder past Frăteşti L and through **Daia** (11km, 30m) (accommodation, refreshments).

Cross railway bridge in village, then start ascending. Take care, there is no hard shoulder on the bridge. Bear R at roundabout (Dn41) (sp Olteniţa) leaving main road and continue ascending onto river terrace, reaching **Plopşoru** (13.5km, 85m) at top of escarpment. Between Plopşoru and **Daita** (14.5km, 87m) road drops down slightly to cross shallow river valley, then does so again after Daita this time zig-zagging down into valley, before climbing gently back onto plateau. Continue through fields and across railway level crossing to reach **Frasin** (17.5km, 91m).

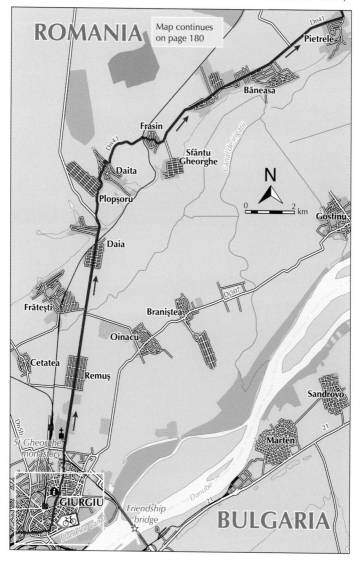

Map continues on page 180

ROMANIA

Dn41

Pietrele

Băneasa

Frasin

Dn47

Sfântu Gheorghe

Daita

Canal de irigatii

Plopşoru

N

0   2 km

Daia

Gostinu

Frăteşti

Braniştea

Dn507

Oinacu

Cetatea

Remuş

Sandrovo

Dn5b

St Gheorghe monastery

Marten

21

GIURGIU

Friendship bridge

Danube

21

Plantelor Canal

BULGARIA

Entrance to Comana natural park

The **railway line** crossed two times is a remnant of the first line opened in Romania (1869), which ran from Bucharest to Giurgiu. The line lost its through service when a bridge over the river Argeş collapsed in 2005. Work on a new bridge commenced in 2021 as part of an EU project to upgrade the rail link between Romania and Bulgaria.

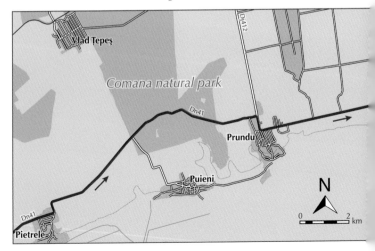

Follow winding asphalt road that undulates through village and continue through fields across plateau to pass through very long spread-out village of **Băneasa** (21km, 93m).

After next village of **Pietrele** (26.5km, 89m), road zigzags L and R into open country before entering thick forest of **Comana natural park**. Established in 2004, there are many bird, plant, mammal and reptile species here. Of particular note are wildcats, otter, water snakes and unique kinds of peony and thorn bush. After 4km, emerge from forest and continue through fields to beginning of **Prundu** (38km, 78m), a prosperous and well-kept village where pruned trees and rose bushes line every street.

Bear R at beginning of village then L before centre (do not go into village proper) and continue through fields to **Greaca** (47.5km, 72m) (accommodation, refreshments). Follow asphalt road winding through village into open country. Pass through another short section of Comana natural park then continue along edge of river terrace on undulating road with extensive views over flood plain R. Pass fishing lake L to reach beginning of **Căscioarele** (59km, 23m).

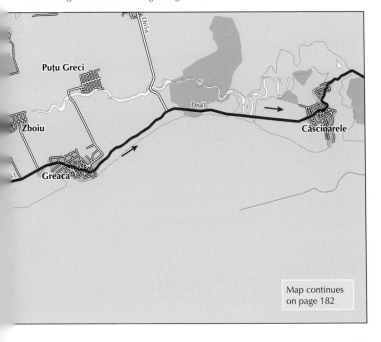

Map continues
on page 182

St Gheorghe modern wooden church in Olteniţa

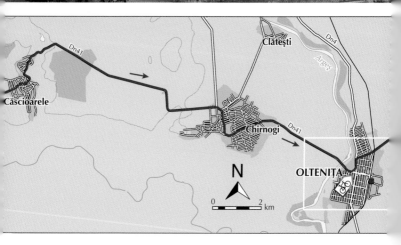

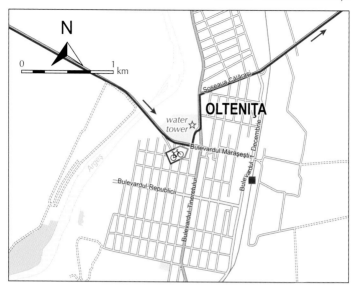

Descend through village to shore of lake Cătălui. Undulate parallel with lake-shore through second part of village crossing another arm of lake, then climb back onto river terrace. After 7km, descend off river terrace again and bear R into **Chirnogi** (70.5km, 23m).

Bear L in middle of village, then follow road out of village through fields with views of Tutrakan (Bulgaria) on hillside on opposite side of Danube. Cross bridge over river Argeş on to Bvd Mărăşeşti to reach end of stage beside central park in **Olteniţa** (76km, 18m) (accommodation, refreshments, station).

Olteniţa (pop. 22,750; was 32,000 in 1992) is located near to the confluence of the Danube with the Argeş, which flows down from the Carpathian mountains. There is a busy port mostly dealing with aggregates and building materials, athough the largest employer, the Navol shipyard, was closed down after being purchased by Mittal Steel.

STAGE 25

Oltenița to Călărași

Start	Oltenița, central park (18m)
Finish	Călărași, Volna church (21m)
Distance	70km
Waymarking	None, follow Dn31

This is the last stage to follow the Danube road and, apart from one short climb onto the river terrace, it is level all the way. The route follows the road along the foot of the terrace through what becomes an almost continuous line of villages, and also crosses a number of man-made lakes. Entry to Călărași is through a post-industrial landscape of a former steelworks.

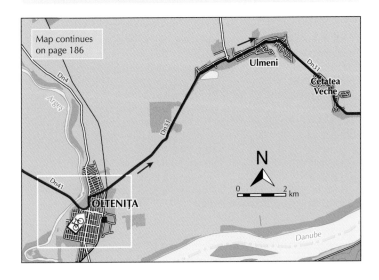

Heroes' monument in centre of Olteniţa

From central park in **Olteniţa**, follow Str Argeşului north. Pass **water-tower** L and bear L on Bvd Tineretului (Dn4). After 300 metres, turn R (Sos Călăraşi, Dn31). Cross railway level crossing and continue into open country. Road climbs gently past disused industrial area onto river terrace to reach **Ulmeni** (9km, 34m), which stretches out along escarpment edge overlooking flood plain.

Follow asphalt road curving R and L through village, then continue through fields and descend into **Spanţov** (16.5km, 19m). Continue, with river terrace always present beside road L to reach **Chiselet** (24km, 19m). The road passes through open fields and into **Mânăstirea** (30km, 17m) (refreshments).

Mânăstirea (pop. 5100), which sits beside lake Mostiştea, a man-made lake behind an earth dam, was an important centre for the fishing industry. Fish from the Danube and many lakes and fishponds on the flood plain were traded at a weekly market and despatched along 'fish roads' for consumption in Bucharest to the north and Bulgaria in the south. St Dumitru church (1648) is one of the oldest in the area.

Muzeul Alexandru Sahia is the birthplace of a 20th-century Romanian socialist writer who was born in 1908. After dropping out of both university and monastic orders he turned his attention to writing. He visited Soviet Russia in 1935 and wrote eulogising the success of the Soviet revolution. He joined the communist party shortly before his death from tuberculosis in 1937. After the communists came to power in Romania he was declared a posthumous member of the Romanian Academy and a hero of the working class.

Cycle through village and across earth dam holding back **lake Mostiştea**. After sluice gates and derelict hydro-electric power station, continue through **Dorobanţu** (34km, 19m) and on to **Vărăşti** (36km, 18m).

Continue on Str Principală through **Ciocăneşti** (44.5km, 19m), which spreads for 7km along the road and joins directly into **Bogata** (49km, 18m).

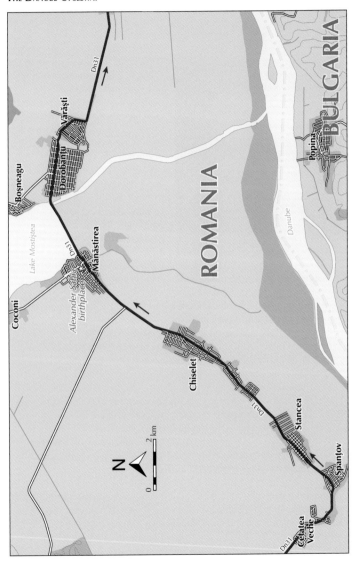

Wayside chapel in Vărăști

Another earth dam, this time over lake Gălățui, leads to **Rasa** (51.5km, 17m), which joins directly into **Cunești** (55km, 17m) and **Grădiștea** (57km, 16m) without any breaks in housing.

Soon after Grădiștea, Călărași steelworks come into view across lagoon R. Short stretch through open fields where road is lined by mature poplars brings

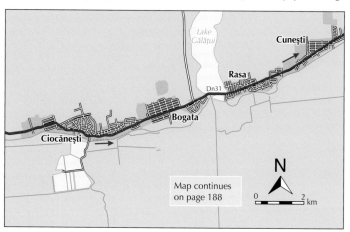

Map continues on page 188

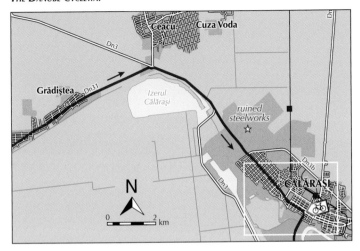

you to road junction with main road from Bucharest (61km, 16m). Turn R onto Dn3 to reach another road junction by sign welcoming you to Călăraşi. Beware, the Dn3 is a busy main road with neither cycle lane nor hard shoulder. Fork L and continue past ruins of former **steelworks** L. After passing more industrial units (working this time) go ahead at roundabout on dual carriageway Str Prelungirea Bucureşti and continue through area of mostly Soviet era buildings. When area of older buildings is reached and dual carriageway ends, street becomes Str Bucureşti and leads into centre of **Călăraşi** (70km, 21m) (accommodation, refreshments, cycle shop, station) where stage ends at traffic lights between **Volna church** L and **courthouse** R.

Călăraşi (pop. 58,000) sits beside the Borcea branch of the Danube, just below the point where it splits from the main river. During the 18th century the small village of Lichireşti became an important staging point for *călăraşii ştafetari* (relay riders) on the route between Istanbul and Bucharest, and as the village grew it became known as the town of the călăraşii. On the front line between Romania and Ottoman Turkish-held Bulgaria, Călăraşi saw frequent conflict during the Russo-Turkish wars causing much destruction. What few old buildings survived were mostly demolished during the communist era, when the city underwent a rapid period of industrial redevelopment, including construction of a steelworks. Much of this industry has closed since 1989 and the population has fallen from 77,000 (1992) to 58,000 (2021). Principal

Ruins of derelict steelworks at Călărași

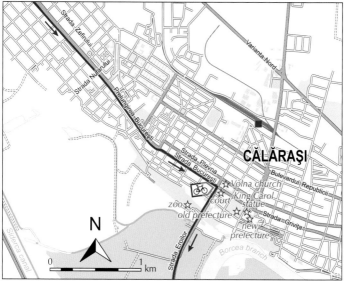

sights include the Italianate-style former prefecture building (1897), several old churches and a cathedral. The equestrian statue of ex-King Carol I is a recent addition to the townscape, being unveiled in 2008. The poorly funded zoo has a collection of animals including tigers, jaguars and bears, while the Dunarea de Jos (Lower Danube) museum concentrates on archaeological finds from the region.

STAGE 26
Călăraşi to Ion Corvin

Start	Călăraşi, Volna church (21m)
Finish	Ion Corvin, Dj223 junction (70m)
Distance	65km
Waymarking	None, follow Dn3

This stage involves a ferry crossing over the Danube and then continues on a quiet main road skirting the border of Bulgaria through the rolling sandy hills of southern Dobruja. There are frequent ascents and descents.

From junction of Str Bucureşti and Str Eroilor beside **Volna church** in centre of Călăraşi, follow Str Eroilor south-west passing **courthouse** L. Very soon road leaves city through woodland, then crosses Siderca canal and curves L to reach roundabout. Take first exit (Dn3) and continue past Albatros Hotel L to reach **Chiciu** ferry ramp (9km, 14m) (accommodation, refreshments). Two ferry services operate from Chiciu. The first goes to Ostrov (Romania) every 15mins. Further on, beyond the Romanian border post, a less frequent ferry goes to Silistra (Bulgaria).

Frequent ferries run between Chiciu and Ostrov near to the Bulgarian city of Silistra

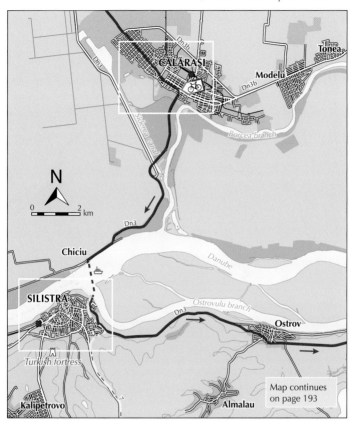

Cross Danube by ferry to Ostrov. Ferry terminal is called Ostrov by the Romanians, even though it is in Romanian part of Silistra, 9km before village of Ostrov. From ferry ramp follow road bearing L (Dn3) parallel with **Romania–Bulgaria border**, passing Bulgarian border crossing point R. Our route does not enter Bulgaria, but you can pop across the border into Silistra [Силистра] (accommodation, refreshments, cycle shop, station) for a short visit to another country.

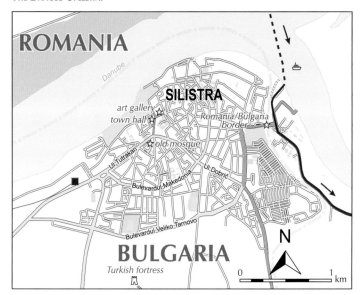

Silistra (pop. 30,000) was the site of an earlier Thracian settlement where the Romans built a garrison called Durostorum as headquarters of the XI legion, which was based here from AD104 for over 350 years. This developed into a Roman city that passed to the Byzantines after the fall of the Roman Empire. It became part of the first Bulgarian Empire towards the end of the seventh century before being captured by the Ottomans in about 1400 and remaining Turkish for nearly 500 years. A large Turkish fort was built in the mid-19th century, but was captured by the Russians during the Russo-Turkish war. After periods of Bulgarian (1878–1913) and Romanian (1913–1940) rule, Silistra became part of modern Bulgaria in 1940. Under communist control, the city developed rapidly as an industrial centre with a population growing to 71,000 by 1989, although this has halved as industry collapsed after the fall of communism. Places of interest include an ancient mosque, municipal buildings grouped around attractive central gardens and the Turkish fort, which stands on a hilltop overlooking the city.

Continue out of town and follow main road climbing through vineyards and orchards onto river terrace. Pass turn-off L for **Ostrov** (16.5km, 28m) (accommodation, refreshments) and continue ascending to pass above village with extensive

Dervent monastery

views of Ostrovulu branch of Danube and islands between this branch and main river. Descend past turn-off for the fishing resort village of **Bugeac** on shore of lake Bugeacului which can be seen R. Pass a series of fishing lakes to reach **Dervent monastery** (Mănăstirea Dervent) L (27.5km, 34m). Take care of your possessions while visiting the monastery as vagrant children often hang around the car park begging and sometimes stealing from visitors. You are allowed to take bicycles inside for safety.

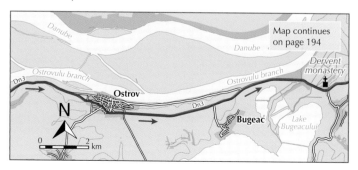

Map continues on page 194

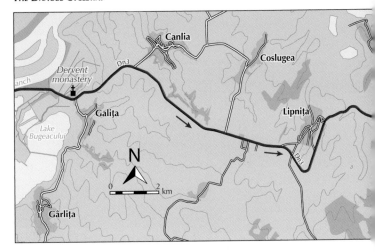

Dervent monastery was constructed at the beginning of the 20th century on the site of an alleged miracle accredited to the apostle Andrew, who is said to have stuck his staff in the ground during a dry period and brought forth water. A spring in the walnut orchard 300 metres from the monastery is believed to flow with healing water. The church attracts large numbers of pilgrims who visit to pray to an icon of the Virgin Mary with miraculous powers and see four stone crosses erected to commemorate four of Andrew's disciples who were martyred nearby. The monastery was closed for 40 years during the communist period, reopening in 1990. A large new church has been built behind the original one.

Climb steeply for 2km onto plateau and cycle through area of orchards and vineyards. Road undulates gently across plateau then descends past **Lipnița** L (41.5km, 103m) (accommodation). Route crosses causeway past head of small lake and ascends into **Băneasa** (51km, 96m) (accommodation, refreshments, tourist office) along short section (1.25km) of cobbles.

Follow main road bearing L in village (sp Constanța) and continue ascending to reach summit (165m) after end of village, then descend steadily through woods into **Negureni** (58km, 62m) (accommodation, refreshments) and ascend a little to **Ion Corvin** (65km, 70m) (accommodation, refreshments) where stage ends at road junction with Dj223 at far end of village.

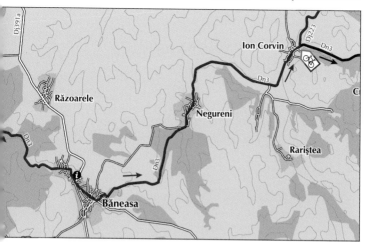

ALTERNATIVE ROUTES THROUGH DOBRUJA

After Ion Corvin you have a decision to make. The official route of EV6 and the Danube cycleway turns north through a remote region of eastern Dobruja. With forward planning this is achievable by almost all cyclists, although there are frequent ascents and long distances between accommodation and refreshment opportunities. An alternative route continues east, taking a direct line to the Black Sea at Constanţa, then turns north along the coast to reach the Danube Delta at Tulcea. This is also hilly, but there are more facilities along the route. This route is summarised as an alternative after Stage 32. Distance from Ion Corvin to Tulcea via main route is 290km while that via Constanţa is 223km.

STAGE 27
Ion Corvin to Cernavodă

Start	Ion Corvin, Dj223 junction (70m)
Finish	Cernavodă, roundabout (17m)
Distance	40.5km
Waymarking	None, follow Dj223

Descending from the southern Dobruja hills, the route follows the Danube then crosses the Danube–Black Sea canal to end in Cernavodă. It is hilly at the beginning and at the end with a flat section in the middle.

From road junction on edge of **Ion Corvin** fork L onto Dj223 (sp Cernavodă) and ascend steadily over ridge, then descend winding through woods into **Floriile** (4km, 81m). Climb back onto plateau (seven per cent gradient) past scrub and vineyard covered hillsides then descend into **Aliman** (10km, 48m), bearing R to follow one-way system winding through village.

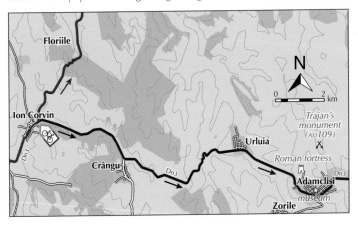

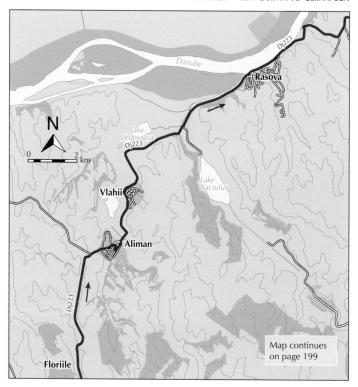

Continue on road to **Vlahii** (13km, 14m) then follow swampy margins of lake Vederoasa to emerge on Danube riverside and cycle past **Rasova** (21.5km, 12m). This is one of very few places in Romania where the road runs alongside the Danube and it is a popular recreational area at weekends. Climb over another ridge and descend into **Cochirleni** (30.5km, 22m).

Road ascends steeply out of village then undulates over another ridge planted with extensive vineyards. Eventually descend from plateau, with view of Cernavodă nuclear power station below R. Bear L to pass under motorway then go ahead at roundabout and continue under railway bridge. Turn L (Str Constantei), then R opposite station (Str Gării) over Podul St Maria bridge high above **Danube– Black Sea canal** into **Cernavodă** (40.5km, 17m) where stage ends at roundabout immediately after bridge (accommodation, refreshments, tourist office, station).

The Anghel Saligni bridges connect Cernavodă
and Fetești across the Danube

DANUBE BRIDGES AND CANALS

Linking Cernavodă and Fetești, a series of impressive bridges carry railway and
motorway over both arms of the Danube. The first two bridges, the Anghel
Saligni railway bridges (formerly King Carol I bridges), were opened in 1895.
When built they were the longest bridges in Europe and third longest in the
world with a combined length of over 4km. The first bridge crosses the main
branch of the river 30m above the water with a lifting section to allow large
vessels to reach the Danube from the Danube–Black Sea canal. The two
bridges are linked by a 14km combined viaduct and causeway across an
island between the river branches. In 1987 the Cernavodă and Fetești bridges
were opened parallel to the Saligni bridges carrying motorway, railway and
walkway/cycleway across both arms of the river. The railway was diverted
across these new bridges and the old Saligni bridges are no longer used.

Plans to build a canal between Cernavodă and Constanța, which
would reduce the distance to the Black Sea by 270km and avoid the

navigational difficulties of the Danube Delta, were first mooted in the 19th century. However, construction of the Danube–Black Sea canal did not begin until 1949 and was not completed until 1984. It was a major engineering project requiring the removal of nearly 400 million cubic metres of spoil (more than either Suez or Panama canals) and construction of four gigantic locks capable of taking sea-going vessels. Initially the work was notorious for the use of forced labour by the communist regime in Romania who established labour camps for up to a million political prisoners set to work with picks and shovels instead of modern machinery. Many died (estimates vary widely between 10,000 and 200,000) from malnutrition, overwork, disease and industrial accidents. Work stopped in 1953 and did not resume again until 1973, this time with skilled labour and proper equipment. The final cost of US$2billion will never be paid off as the canal generates an income of only US$4million annually.

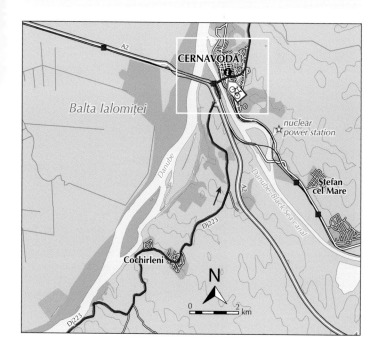

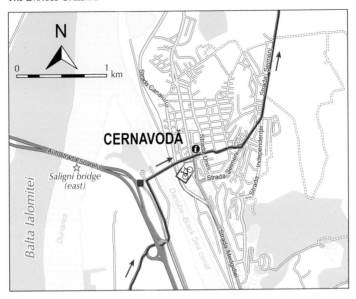

The Danube–Black Sea canal at Cernavodă

STAGE 28
Cernavodă to Hârşova

Start	Cernavodă, roundabout (17m)
Finish	Hârşova, Dn22a junction (32m)
Distance	53km
Waymarking	None, follow Dj223

The route continues north, parallel with the Danube, on a quiet road through a series of small villages beside the river terrace. There are no large hills but the route does climb on and off the river terrace eight times with a total ascent of over 600m making this the hilliest stage of all.

From roundabout in **Cernavodă**, go straight ahead uphill (Str Crişan). Dogleg R and L and continue uphill on Str 24 Ianuarie. Turn L at T-junction (Str Seimeni, Dn223) continuing out of town and over summit (87m). Descend to cross river bridge and pass **Seimenii Mici** (6km, 18m) (accommodation, refreshments). Climb back onto plateau and turn R (sp Constanţa) to by-pass **Seimeni** (7km, 67m).

Continue across plateau for 3km, with view of Seimeni and Danube below L, then turn sharply L (sp Dunărea), dropping downhill to Danube. Continue to **Dunărea** (15.5km, 29m). Climb through village, then descend again and climb over small ridge to reach **Capidava** (22.5km, 18m) (accommodation, refreshments, camping) passing ruined **castle** on riverside L.

The ruined castle at **Capidava** dates from Roman times. The Romans reached the Danube in Dobruja in AD14. In AD46 a small Roman garrison was established near to an old Dacian settlement at Capidava, probably intended to control a ford over the river. This was expanded into a castle on a rocky massif above the river by Trajan as part of his preparations to invade Dacia in AD101. The fortress had 500 metres of two-metre-thick walls with seven towers over 10m tall. There were two gates, one of which led down to a port beside the Danube. A natural moat ran around the landward side of the fortress. Destroyed by the Goths in the third century, it was subsequently rebuilt before being abandoned by the Romans in AD559. The Byzantines rebuilt the site as a fortified town, which was finally destroyed by fire in 1036. Archaeological research, which started in 1924, has yielded many Roman remains including two graveyards with altars and funerary monuments.

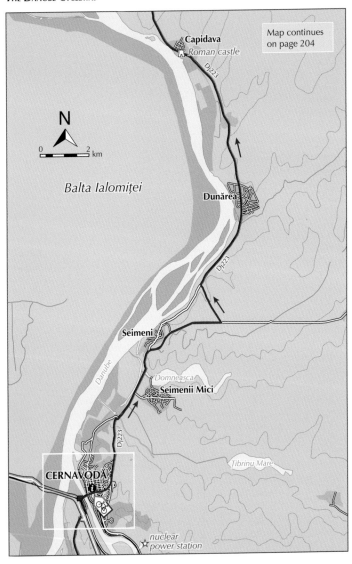

Map continues
on page 204

Capidava
Roman castle

Dj223

N
0   2 km

Balta Ialomiţei

Dunărea

Dj223

Seimeni

Danube

Domneasca

Seimenii Mici

Dj223

Tibrinu Mare

CERNAVODĂ

*nuclear
power station*

Ruins of Capidava Roman fortress

Climb back onto plateau passing vine-covered slopes L, then descend into **Topalu** (29.5km, 35m). Turn R in village (Str Hirsovei) and climb steadily into open country, then descend towards Tichileşti. By sign at beginning of **Tichileşti** (36km, 15m) turn L on poorly surfaced country road (sp Ghindăreşti) avoiding village. Climb steadily onto river terrace again then drop down and follow road winding through **Ghindăreşti** (43.5km, 14m). Climb back onto river terrace and continue across plateau to reach main road. Turn L on Dn2a to reach large filling station (refreshments) at road junction just before **Hârşova** (53km, 32m) (accommodation, refreshments). To reach accommodation and refreshment options bear L through Hârşova and continue to the far end of town. To continue on to Stage 29, turn sharply R on Dn22a.

Hârşova (pop. 8700) was established by the Romans as a fortress called Carsium overlooking the Danube. Later the Ottoman Turks built a castle on the site, which, although garrisoned by 2000 men, was captured by the Russians during the Russo-Turkish wars.

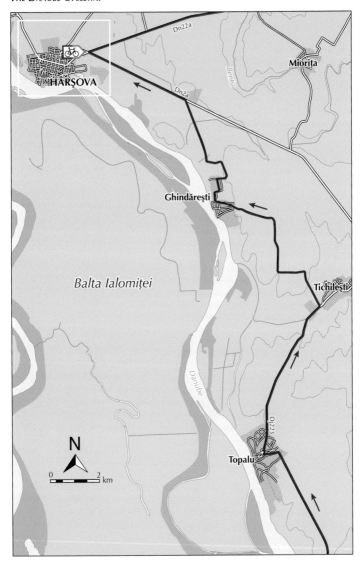

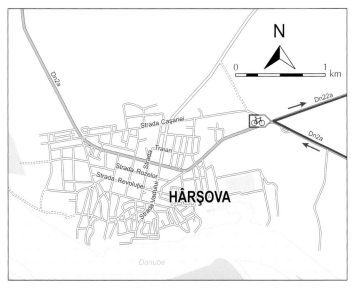

Hârșova parish church

STAGE 29
Hârşova to Măcin

Start	Hârşova, Dn22a junction (32m)
Finish	Măcin, Dn22 junction (22m)
Distance	88km
Waymarking	None, follow Dj222f, then Dn22d

This stage continues north on quiet roads undulating on and off the river terrace following the Măcin branch of the Danube through a number of small impoverished villages. After Cerna the foothills of the Măcin mountains are crossed, before descending into Măcin.

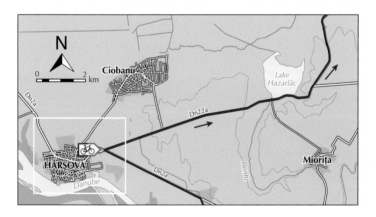

From main road junction by filling station east of Hârşova take Dn22a heading north-east (sp Saraiu) ascending gently across plateau. Descend to pass **lake Hazarlâc** L, then climb again and fork L on undulating country road (sp Gârliciu Dn222f) passing area of swampy marshland R. Pass a place where road runs along edge of river terrace (15km, 24m) and landslip has caused road to subside and be replaced with short diversion away from affected area. Continue into **Gârliciu**

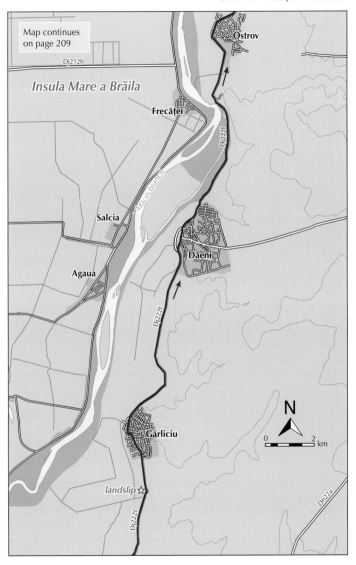

Map continues
on page 209

Dj212b

Insula Mare a Brăila

Frecăţei

Dj222f

Ostrov

Măcin branch

Salcia

Dăeni

Agaua

Dj222f

Gârliciu

landslip ☆

Dj222f

N

0   2 km

Dn22a

The granite peaks of the Măcin mountains are the oldest in Romania

(17.5km, 35m). Follow asphalt road winding through village, then descend to continue on narrow strip of Danube flood plain, with river terrace rising R. Where Daeni by-pass forks L, continue ahead into **Dăeni** (26.5km, 9m). Fork L towards end of village (sp Măcin) and continue to reach **Ostrov** (35.5km, 8m).

Pass below village and continue along edge of flood plain for 8km. Climb over a ridge (summit 113m) and descend round a series of bends passing through edge of **Peceneaga** (48km, 5m). Turn R and climb back onto river terrace then continue across plateau and descend into **Traian** (56.5km, 9m). Turn L at beginning of village, following road (now Dj222b) climbing gently to reach **Cerna** (65km, 51m). Turn L in village on undulating Dn22d (sp Măcin) then ascend steadily through open country to reach summit (152m), with view of Măcin mountains ahead. The Dn22d is a busy main road with neither cycle lane nor hard shoulder.

Although as mountains go, the **Măcin mountains**, which rise to the right of our route between Cerna and Măcin, are not very high, they are the oldest mountains in Romania. Formed of granite, which has eroded in castle-like crags, the highest point is **Țuțuiatu Greci** (467m). Partly forested and partly covered by steppe scrub, the mountains have been declared a national park, well-known for the wide variety of bird species to be seen, particularly the European turtle dove and long-legged buzzard.

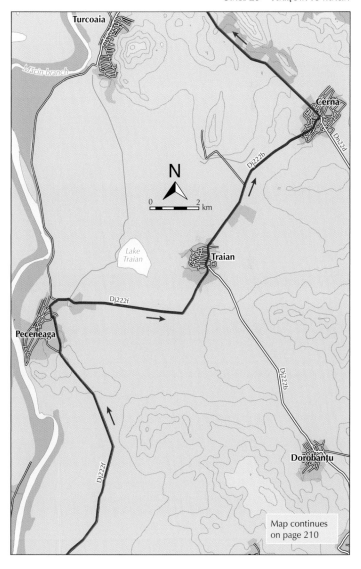

Map continues on page 210

After two short sections of cobbles, descend past turn-offs for Turcoaia L and Greci R (refreshments, camping) and continue into **Măcin** (88km, 22m) (accommodation, refreshments, tourist office) where stage ends at junction with Dn22.

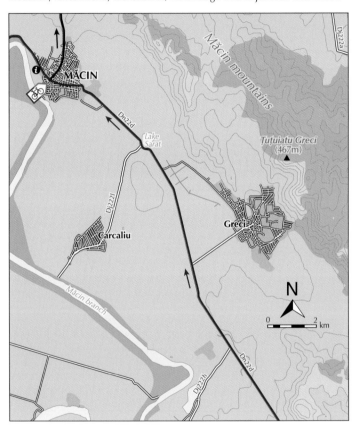

STAGE 30
Măcin to Galați

Start	Măcin, Dn22 junction (22m)
Finish	Galați, ferry ramp (7m)
Distance	30km
Waymarking	None, follow Dn22 then Dn22b

The main route follows a short level ride along a quiet road before crossing the river by ferry to Brăila. After another short level section, this time along a busy main road, you reach the industrial city of Galați.

ALTERNATIVE ROUTE BY-PASSING BRĂILA AND GALAȚI
Turn R in middle of **Măcin** onto Str Florilor Dn22 (sp Tulcea) and head north past foothills of Măcin mountains to **Jijila** (7km, 16m) and on to join Stage 31 by turning R at edge of **Garvăn** (12.5km, 11m). This shortens the route by 30km.

From **Măcin** continue west downhill out of town following Dn22 parallel with Măcin branch of Danube behind trees L. Where road bears R towards Brăila suspension bridge, turn L (sp Smârdan) and continue along flood dyke to reach beginning of Smârdan. Where main road bears R, continue ahead (Str Preot Stefan Carlan; no entry but entry permitted for cyclists) through village to reach **Smârdan** ferry ramp (12.5km, 4m) and cross river by ferry to **Brăila**. Ferry operates hourly, 24hrs a day. From Brăila ferry ramp, cycle ahead for 1km, then bear R to reach road junction.

Excursion to Brăila
To visit Brăila (accommodation, refreshments, camping, tourist office, cycle shop, station) turn L and follow Bvd Dorobanților over railway bridge. After 1.25km, turn L at traffic lights (Calea Galați) to reach city centre.

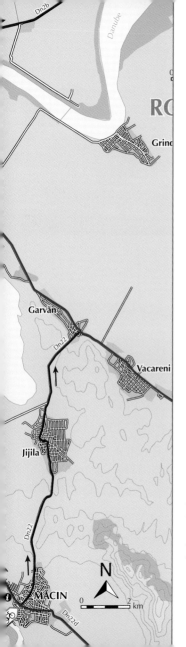

Brăila (pop. 155,000) is a major port and industrial city that can trace its origins back to 14th-century Wallachia. Captured by the Ottomans in 1538 it remained in Turkish hands until 1829. The late 19th–early 20th century was a period of rapid economic development which led to Brăila becoming the third largest Romanian inland port. Forced industrial factory development during the communist years saw the population rise from 95,000 (1948) to 234,000 (1992), with most newcomers accommodated in large suburban estates of concrete residence blocks. As many of these factories closed after the fall of communism, the population fell to 155,000 (2021).

The city is laid out with radial streets running away from the old port and orbital streets looping around the city centre; it is unusual for Romania in that much of the old centre has been preserved. Most of the main tourist sights are concentrated around Piața Traian, the central square in the old town, where you will find a statue of Roman Emperor Trajan, the Mary Filotti Theatre, City museum and ornamental clock tower. Nearby is the Church of the Archangels Greek Orthodox church. The modern centre around Piața Independenței has the town hall, Palace of culture and Esplanade gardens with a series of fountains and access to a riverside walkway.

213

Piaţa Independenţei fountains in Brăila give a spectacular light show at night

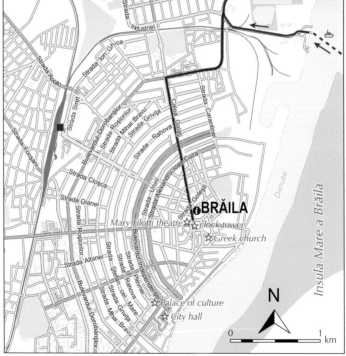

Main route continues to Galați

Turn R on busy main road, with no cycle lane, that runs along flood dyke out of city with open fields L and riparian woodland R to reach roundabout under Brăila suspension bridge. The Brăila suspension bridge, which opened in 2023, is the third longest in the EU. Turn R (first exit sp Galați sud). After 8km, cross railway level crossing and pass extensive coal port R. Cross conveyor belt taking coal from port to Galați steelworks and continue over river Siret, passing campus of Galați Danubius private university R. Enter Galați on Bvd Galați ascending steeply through area of Soviet era housing blocks. Go straight ahead at first roundabout, then bear R at next much larger roundabout, with orange tower in middle, into Str Oțelarilor on cycle track R. At T-junction at end of street follow cycle track bearing R (Str Prelungirea Saturn). At next T-junction turn L sharply downhill. The road on the R leads to a TV tower with a lift to the viewing gallery. Turn R at next roundabout then bear R to reach ferry ramp in **Galați** (30km, 7m) (accommodation, refreshments, tourist office, cycle shop, station).

GALAȚI

Galați (pop. 218,000) is a major port and industrial city with a very attractive riverside promenade. The Romans built a fortress at Baboși (just south of where the enormous Arcelor-Mittal steelworks now stands) to defend a ford at the junction of Siret and Danube rivers. Later the Byzantines developed a small town, which became briefly a Genoese colony in the 15th century.

Captured by the Ottoman Turks in 1484, it was the main trading port of Moldova, particularly for grain and timber. During the 18th- and 19th-century Russo-Turkish wars, Galați became a Turkish naval base with a shipyard for building large warships; however, its frontline position led to its capture and burning by the Russians on several occasions.

After becoming part of Romania in 1859, trade grew and a number of lavish former merchants' houses attest to a period of prosperity. The shipyard expanded, railways arrived and factories opened. Growth

Precista fortified monastery in Galați has a secret escape tunnel to the Danube

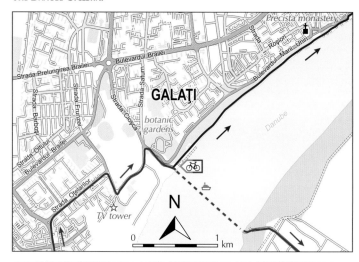

slowed between the world wars and during the Second World War the city was badly damaged by both Soviet Russian and Nazi German bombing that destroyed many old buildings. After the war Galați was rebuilt on communist lines with forced industrialisation and a large number of Soviet style housing blocks. The biggest development was Romania's largest steelworks operated by Sidex. This is still open and since 2002 has been owned by Arcelor Mittal. The population grew from 80,000 (1948) to 326,000 (1992), but has since fallen to 218,000 (2021).

Tourist sights include the fortified Mănăstirea Precista monastery of the Holy Virgin (1647), the oldest building in Galați. Built in stone, brick and wood, it has a watchtower and defensive battlements, together with an escape tunnel to the Danube. There are a number of parks and gardens (the city claims to be the greenest in Romania) including the botanic gardens.

There are two alternative routes between Galați and Isaccea, both requiring a short ferry crossing. Stage 31 describes a route by the south bank which starts with a ferry and stays entirely within Romania, while Stage 31A is a north bank route that passes through Moldova and Ukraine before ending with a ferry back to Romania.

STAGE 31
Galați to Isaccea (through Romania)

Start	Galați, ferry ramp (7m)
Finish	Isaccea, mosque (11m)
Distance	42km
Waymarking	None, follow Dn22e then Dn22

After crossing the river by ferry, there is an undulating ride along quiet main roads between the Danube flood plain and the rolling sandy foothills of the Măcin mountains to reach the small town of Isaccea.

From ferry ramp in **Galați**, take ferry (0600–2200; every 30mins) across Danube to **I.C.Brătianu**. Follow road (Dn22e) through village and into open country, crossing Danube flood plain on a long causeway with view of Măcin mountains R. Climb gently round edge of range of low hills, passing above ruins of **Cetatea Dinogetia** Roman fortress L (9.5km, 20m).

Ruins of Dinogetia Roman fortress

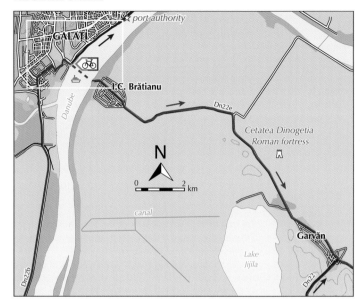

Cetatea Dinogetia was a Dacian settlement conquered by the Romans at the beginning of the first century AD, who built a boundary fortress on a bluff overlooking the Danube flood plain. Its importance increased when the Romans withdrew from Dacia (the left bank of the Danube) in AD275 and the fortifications were strengthened to combat barbarian invaders. Archaeological research has uncovered Roman housing, a bath house, basilica and graveyard surrounded by a wall that was three-metres thick and had 14 defensive towers. Badly damaged by the Avars in AD559, it was later rebuilt by the Byzantines before being abandoned finally in 1186. The site can be visited, but is mostly overgrown.

Continue through **Garvăn** (13km, 8m) to reach road junction just before end of village. The alternative route from Măcin rejoins at the road junction. Bear L (Dn22) and skirt northern foothills of Măcin mountains to reach **Văcăreni** (16.5km, 16m).

Road then climbs steeply (gradient 10 per cent) over small ridge (summit 64m) before descending through **Luncaviţa** (25km, 18m) (accommodation, refreshments).

Short stretch of open country precedes ascent through small village of **Rachelu** (29km, 33m), situated on a bluff above flood plain L. Undulating road then winds along sandy hillside keeping above swampy margins of lake Crapina L to reach **Revărsarea** (36km, 17m).

On the last bend before Revărsarea, a sign points uphill to **Tichileşti** hospital, the last remaining leper colony in Romania. In this remote community nine elderly leprosy sufferers live an isolated and quiet life, all that remain of 185 patients in 1946. During the communist period, Romania was declared 'free' of leprosy, and to make this appear so, Tichileşti was 'removed' from official maps. Although modern medicine allows leprosy to be treated within the community, making isolation hospitals unnecessary, residents at Tichileşti still follow the old ways. The last case of leprosy was diagnosed in 1981, since when no new patients have been admitted.

A low ridge is crossed before road drops down to enter **Isaccea** (42km, 11m) (accommodation, refreshments) on Calea Măcin. Continue round bend R into Str 1 Decembrie 1918 where stage ends beside **mosque**.

Isaccea (pop. 4400) is near the site of a Roman naval base at Noviodunum, the scant remains of which can be found beside the river, 2km east of town. It remained an important Byzantine naval base until AD602. In 1484, Isaccea was captured by the Ottoman Turks, and although most of the Turkish

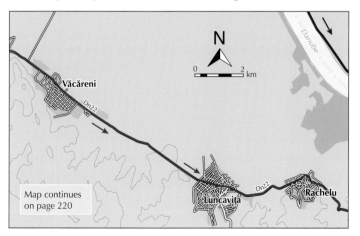

Map continues on page 220

16th-century Azizyie mosque in Isaccea serves a small Turkish congregation of 250 people

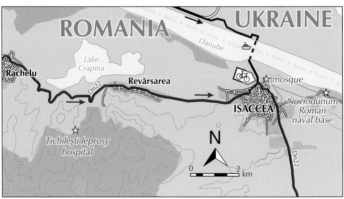

population left after the city became part of Romania (1877), a small Islamic community of about 250 people remain and worship in the 16th-century Azizyie mosque.

STAGE 31A

Galaţi to Isaccea (through Moldova and Ukraine)

At the time of writing, Ukraine is at war with Russia and official warning from the UK foreign office advises against travel in Ukraine. Although the part of Ukraine traversed by this stage is far from the front line, travel should be avoided until the war ends and this advice changes.

Start	Galaţi, ferry ramp (7m)
Finish	Isaccea, mosque (11m)
Distance	52km
Waymarking	None

It is only 15km from the Galaţi ferry ramp to the Romanian border with Moldova and another 3km through Moldova to the Ukrainian border. The centre of Reni [Рени], Ukraine's first town, lies 6km into the country. Another 25km beside the Danube takes you to Orlivka from where a ferry crosses the river to Isaccea. Visas are not needed by EU passport holders but beware, crossing three borders can be time consuming.

From ferry ramp in Galaţi follow cycle track north-east through barrier into riverside park and follow this along riverside promenade (Faleza) for 2.75km with sandy cliffs of river terrace rising L. After second barrier turn L and immediately R (Str Portului) past impressive port administration building R. Bear L at entrance to port (Str Garii Nr 8) crossing series of railway tracks. Turn R at T-junction (Str Alexandru Moruzzi). Just before railway level crossing turn L (Str Lemnasi) over more railway tracks to reach main road. Turn R on Calea Prutului (Dn2b) with cobbled tram tracks down the centre. Cross railway bridge then pass railway yards L and Damen shipyards R. Cross another railway bridge and railway yards R and continue into open country. After 9km reach **Romanian border post** then continue over girder bridge to **Moldovan border post** at **Giurgiuleşti** (16km, 18m). Although you do not need a visa, you will still be required to present your passport and complete immigration formalities.

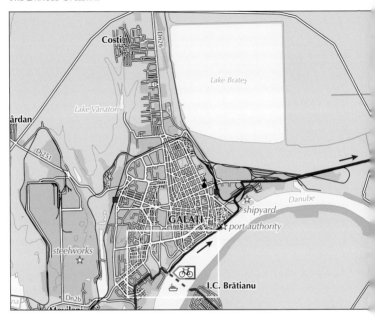

Cycle track along Faleza promenade in Galaţi

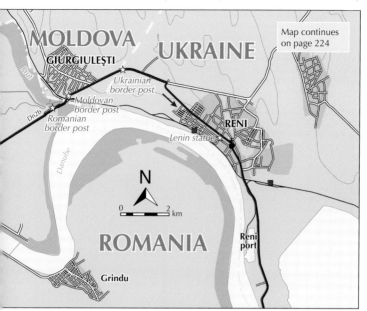

Moldova (pop. 3.1 million) is a small and little known European country that has only had an independent existence since the collapse of the Soviet Union in 1991. Previously it had been part of either Russia or Romania; indeed, the western part of Moldova still is part of Romania and has been since 1859. During the communist period there was a substantial movement of ethnic Russians and Ukrainians into the country and in the eastern region of Transnistria they constitute a majority. When attempts were made during the 1990s to reunite Moldova with Romania, this move was opposed by Russians and Ukrainians and led to a secessionist civil war in Transnistria. Tensions here remain high, but Transnistria is a long way from the area you are visiting. Moldova is Europe's poorest country, with the highest level of emigration. Current policy is to ameliorate these problems by seeking eventual entry into the European Union.

Continue on road, now in poor condition, steadily uphill through Moldova to pass Moldovan exit border post and cross border to reach **Ukrainian border post** (18km, 82m). More formalities to complete before you can cycle downhill

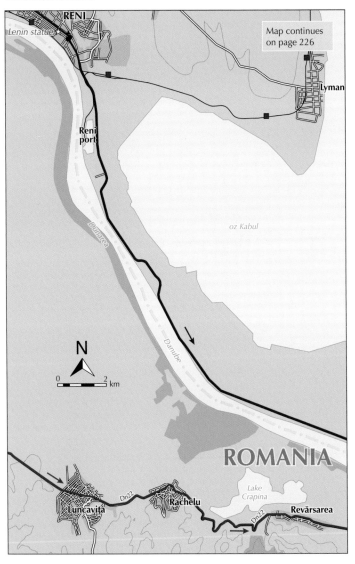

Map continues on page 226

RENI

Lenin statue

Lyman

Reni port

Dunarea

oz Kabul

Danube

N

0   2 km

ROMANIA

Lake Crapina

Dn22

Luncaviţa

Rachelu

Dn22

Revărsarea

Russian Orthodox basilica at Reni in Ukraine

A golden bust of Lenin is displayed in Reni (Ukraine)

to reach outskirts of Reni. Turn R soon after 304km post (ignoring signs pointing ahead) and bear L downhill on badly surfaced side road passing solar farm R and cemetery L. Continue into Ul Komsomolskaya [Ул Комсомольская] past park with golden bust of Lenin R to reach square in centre of **Reni** [Рени] (24km, 15m) (accommodation, refreshments, camping). If you need money in Ukraine it is not possible to change Romanian currency. Take euros or draw money from a cash machine with your bank card.

Reni (pop. 18,000) is a sleepy Ukrainian port town that prior to 1940 was part of Romanian Moldova. After a period of Nazi occupation it was captured by the Russian communists in 1944 and eventually became part of Ukraine. The majority of the Romanian population was

225

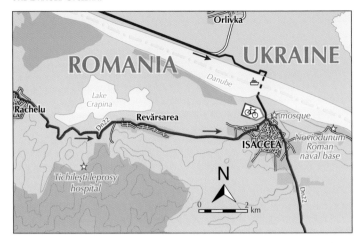

deported to Siberia and replaced with incoming Russians and Ukrainians. The few tourist sights include an Orthodox basilica with golden dome, statue of Lenin in central park and classical style Seamens' Club. The port area, used to export grain, was bombed by the Russians in 2023 during their invasion of Ukraine.

Leave square from southern corner, heading SW on 28 Chervnya vulytsya [28 Червня вулиця]. Follow this out of town, crossing railway and passing industrial area R. Continue ahead on road M-15, passing **Reni port** R and emerge beside Danube. Follow M-15 beside river for 16.5km, to reach point where road turns away from river into Orlivka [Орлівка]. Keep R on minor road beside river, then cross small bridge over sidestream and bear R at triangular junction to reach **Orlivka ferry complex** [Орлівка поромний комплекс] (49.5km, 3m). Ferry operates every three hours, or more frequently depending upon demand, crossing time 10min. www.porom. org, +38 048 406 2516.

Cross Danube by ferry to Isaccea ferry terminal. Pass through Romanian border post, then follow road away from river to beginning of Isaccea. Turn L (Str 1 Decembrie 1918), to reach stage end in front of mosque in Isaccea (52km, 11m).

STAGE 32
Isaccea to Tulcea

Start	Isaccea, mosque (11m)
Finish	Tulcea Oraş station (3m)
Distance	36km
Waymarking	None, follow Dn22

This, the final cyclable stage, continues through the sandy foothills of the Măcin mountains with the Danube flood plain in view below. About halfway the road climbs steeply over a wooded ridge before continuing, undulating all the way, to Tulcea, gateway city for the wetlands of the Danube Delta.

Map continues on page 228

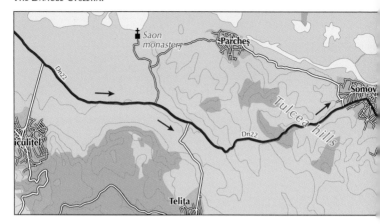

From mosque in centre of **Isaccea**, follow Str 1 Decembrie 1918 (Dn22) south. Continue out of town climbing steadily and pass electricity sub-station R. Cycle through fields and descend to pass turn-off to Mănăstirea Cocos monastery R. Continue through fields to reach turn-off for **Niculiţel** R (10.5km, 42m).

> **Niculiţel** (pop. 3800), on the hillside above the route, is a wine producing village, part of the Sarica-Niculiţel wine region that during communist times produced large quantities of cheap, poor quality wine. Replanting with quality vines of big selling varietals has seen quality improve, and foreign producers have purchased some vineyards. The village is the site of an early Christian basilica that had become buried. It was exposed in 1972 when a heavy storm washed away the covering earth to expose a crypt housing the coffins of four early Christian martyrs. Their coffins are now kept at Mănăstirea Cocos monastery.

Follow road across sandy plateau past gaudy roadside portrait of St Andrew by turn-off for Mănăstirea Saon monastery L and 1.5km further on pass turn-off R to Mănăstirea Celic Dere monastery. Ascend steeply (gradient 10 per cent) through grassy hillside dotted with mature oak trees, to reach summit at 163m. After crossing summit plateau, descend through woodland and fields to reach **Somova** (23.5km, 11m).

> The monasteries of **Cocos**, **Saon** and **Celic Dere** make up a holy triangle in the hills west of Tulcea. All three are attractive complexes of white churches

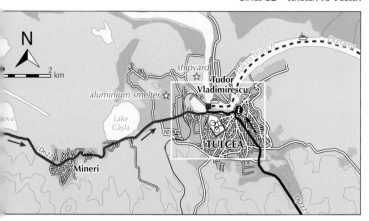

A gaudy image of St Andrew at the turn-off for the Saon monastery

and cloisters, set in wooded locations. Inside they have collections of rare icons, carpets and other decorative items. In addition, Cocos houses the coffins of four Christian martyrs found in Niculițel. Unfortunately none are very close to our route. Cocos and Celic Dere are in the hills to the south. Saon is the easiest reached, being 3km north of and slightly lower than our route.

Follow road turning R in middle of village and passing lake Somova on edge of Danube flood plain. Climb up and over small ridge, then descend winding through **Mineri** (29km, 26m) (accommodation, refreshments).

After end of village, pass earth and stone retaining dam for industrial waste ponds of Tulcea aluminium factory R. Pass under railway bridge and go straight ahead at roundabout (Str Isaccei). Pass industrial area L then cross railway level crossing and pass lake Ciuperca L. Go straight ahead over next roundabout and at third roundabout by end of lake turn L to reach **Tulcea** Oraș station and nearby boat quays for ferries to the Danube Delta (36km, 3m) (accommodation, refreshments, tourist office, cycle shop, station). To reach Tulcea city centre, go straight ahead at the third roundabout and continue for one kilometre.

The Independence monument overlooks Tulcea from monument hill

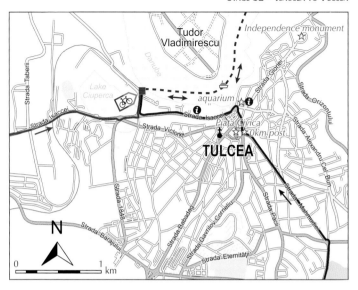

Tulcea (pop. 66,000), a city built on seven low hills, was founded by the Dacians (as Aegyssus) in the fourth century BC. Captured and fortified by the Romans, it subsequently passed through Byzantine, Genoese and Ottoman hands before becoming part of Romania in 1878. Soviet era development changed the city from a rural backwater to an industrial and commercial city with a shipyard and an aluminium factory. Tourist sights in the city include the Danube Delta ecological museum with an aquarium in the basement dedicated to the fish of the delta, two cathedrals plus various churches, a mosque and a synagogue. On monument hill, north-east of the centre is the Independence monument and the remains of Aegyssus Roman fortress.

Tulcea is known as the 'Gateway to the Delta'. Modern hotels and house-boats cater for visitors coming and going from the delta. Boats and ferries from the quay serve delta towns and villages, many of which can only be reached by water.

231

STAGE 32A

Tulcea to Sulina by boat through the Danube Delta

Start	Tulcea, quayside (3m)
Finish	Sulina, Black Sea beach (0m)
Distance	147km (round trip)

There are few roads in the Danube Delta, so the only way to reach the point where the Danube ends and enters the Black Sea is to leave your cycle behind (or take it on the ferry) for a river borne excursion to visit the mouth of the Danube.

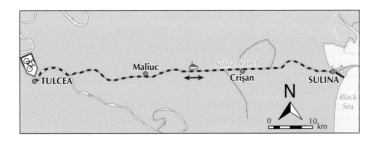

THE DANUBE DELTA

The Danube enters the Black Sea via the Danube Delta, a 4150sqkm area of wetlands that is a UNESCO World Heritage Site. Sediment brought down by the river is expanding the delta into the Black Sea by about 40 metres per year. Water flows through the delta in three main channels, the Chilia branch in the north which takes over half the flow and forms the border between Romania and Ukraine, the Sulina arm in the centre, partly cana-lised and used by shipping, and the St Gheorghe arm in the south. Between these arms are a myriad of smaller waterways and lagoons, the courses of which are constantly changing. Only one fifth of the area is solid ground, the rest is wetland and marsh. Ornithologists have identified 274 species of bird either breeding or migrating through the delta, of which the white pelican, a summer breeding migrant from Egypt, is the most emblematic. Wild animals and reptiles include snakes, otter, mink and wild boar living in a landscape with a wide diversity of trees and plants.

The 15,000 human inhabitants traditionally made a living from fishing, although during the communist era attempts were made to develop agriculture with large areas being cleared for reed cultivation. Nowadays tourism is the main industry. Among these inhabitants are a community of Lipovans (Russian Old Believers) who fled to the delta to escape religious persecution in 18th-century Russia. There are very few roads and transport is almost exclusively by boat. It is possible to explore the many backwaters, but if you do so it is essential to take a local guide. To enter the more ecologically sensitive areas that are part of the Delta Biosphere Reserve it is necessary to obtain a permit from the reserve administration (ARBDD) in Tulcea (Str Portului 34A, 0800–1600, Monday–Friday).

At Tulcea you have gone as far as you can go on your bicycle, but it is still 71km from here through the Danube Delta to the point where the Danube reaches the Black Sea. Having come all this way it would be a pity to miss the final lap to the ocean. Traditional ferries (four hours) or catamarans (three hours), which depart from the quayside near the railway station, link Tulcea with Sulina near the end of the canalised Sulina arm of the river. Mosquitoes and insects are a problem in summer so make sure you have a supply of insect repellent.

BOAT SERVICES

Traditional ferries operated by Navrom depart daily at 1330, returning from Sulina at 0700 the next morning. Catamarans, with limited cycle space, leave at 1000 on Friday/Saturday/Sunday and return from Sulina at 1330. There are also services to other Delta destinations, and private ferries and tour boats offer a variety of excursions. Navrom fares are fixed but private operators' prices are often negotiable. Details available from www.navromdelta.ro.

Ferries call at a number of intermediate piers including **Maliuc** (25km), a communist era planned development as a centre for the reed collecting industry, and **Crişan** (47km) (accommodation, refreshments), an old fishing village, now mostly a tourist centre with guest houses and pensions.

Danube zero km marker in Sulina

The ferry ends at **Sulina** (71km, 0m) (accommodation, refreshments). To reach the Black Sea, head away from ferry quay (Str Duiliu Zamfirescu) beside children's playground R and turn L on concrete block road (sp Plaja Sulina). Fork R (Str Nicolae Bălcescu) by old **lighthouse** and head out of town across sand flats. Pass international graveyard R and reach sandy **beach** with bars and bathing pier (2.5km from quay). Take a dip in the Black Sea, you deserve it!

Sulina (pop. 3100), which was once a prosperous port and shipyard, nowadays relies heavily on tourism. For the cycle tourist who has reached here following the Danube the most interesting sights are the Danube 0km marker (across the river from the Navrom ferry quay surrounded by old ships that are being broken up) and the old lighthouse. The graveyard in the dunes has gravestones from 25 different nationalities including a section for British seafarers who died in marine accidents in the delta.

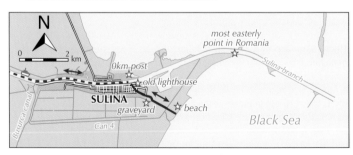

VARIANT FOR STAGES 27–32

Ion Corvin to Tulcea via Constanța

Start	Ion Corvin, Dj223 junction (65m)
Finish	Tulcea, Oraş station (3m)
Distance	223km
Waymarking	None, follow Dn3, Dc86, Dj226, Dj222

This variant climbs east away from the Danube, undulating frequently over the hills of southern Dobruja to reach the large Black Sea port and resort city of Constanța. It then turns north, roughly following the coast to the Danube Delta along a mixture of flat coastal sections and gentle but frequent climbs inland over rolling hills. Allow three days.

From road junction just outside Ion Corvin, follow Dn3 (sp Constanța) ascending past **Crângu** (4.5km, 123m) to summit at 178m. A descent round series of hairpin bends to **Urluia** (10.5km, 41m) and subsequent climb takes you past remains of Roman fortress and on into **Adamclisi** (14.5km, 114m) (refreshments).

> Roman emperor Trajan erected a 30m-high monument near **Adamclisi** to commemorate Roman victory over the Dacians (AD109). Later Constantine constructed a nearby Roman fortress with 22 towers, four gates, running water and sewerage systems, cobbled streets and four early Christian churches. The complex was destroyed by the Avars (AD587) and not redis-covered for many centuries.

Road now winds and undulates steeply across a plateau through **Deleni** (19km, 93m) and past **Pietreni** (25.5km, 119m). Road straightens, now with smaller undulations, through **Viişoara** (36.5km, 138m), **Cobadin** (39.5km, 125m) (accommodation, refreshments), **Ciocârlia de Jos** (45.5km, 119m) and **Ciocârlia de Sus** (50km, 104m), before passing under motorway and descending through woodland of Fântâniţa nature reserve to reach **Murfatlar** (58km, 20m) (accom-modation, refreshments, tourist office, station).

Cross Danube–Black Sea canal, then bear L and turn R onto busy main road past station R and through **Valu lui Traian** (63.5km, 38m) (accommodation,

Constanța's art noveau style casino was built in 1910

refreshments, station). Road, now an absolutely straight busy tree-lined dual car-riageway, climbs gently for 10km to reach outskirts of Constanța. Continue straight ahead, now descending, through industrial area and past Soviet era housing to reach T-junction. Turn L (Bvd Ferdinand) to reach centre of **Constanța** (78.5km, 37m) (accommodation, refreshments, camping, cycle shop, station).

Formerly a Greek colony called Tomis, **Constanța** (pop. 264,000) was cap-tured (29BC) and developed into a town by the Romans. A number of Roman remains can be seen including a 700-square-metre mosaic. The poet Ovid was banished to Tomis and is said to be buried in Piața Ovidiu. Renamed Constanța after the sister of the emperor Constantine, the town was controlled successively by Byzantines, Bulgarians and Ottoman Turks before becom-ing part of Romania in 1877. As the country's principal seaport, Constanța became an important trading city that grew to become the largest port on the Black Sea. Industrial development during the communist era saw the popula-tion increase from 78,000 (1948) to 350,000 (1992). While maintaining its maritime role, the city is also a major seaside resort, part of the Romanian

Mamaia beach and hotel strip is the most popular holiday destination for Romanian families

Riviera, with a famous casino and a wide choice of hotels, guest houses and restaurants. Other attractions include an Orthodox cathedral, old Genovese lighthouse and House of the Lions former masonic temple. The Mahmudiye mosque is spiritual centre for Romania's 55,000 Muslim population. Its 50m-high minaret can be climbed for a view of the city and harbour.

Head north from Constanța on Bvd Mamaia past lake Tăbăcăriei, then continue (Dc86) on 8km-long but only 300-metre-wide strip of land between lake Siutghiol and Black Sea through **Mamaia** beach resort (84km, 3m) (accommodation, refreshments, camping, cycle shop). At **Năvodari** (95.5km, 4m) (accommodation, camping) bear L over canal and turn R at roundabout (Dj226), then continue past oil refinery to reach **Corbu** (105km, 7m) (accommodation, refreshments, camping). Road, much quieter now, climbs through fields to summit (111m) then descends through **Săcele** (117km, 47m). Dogleg R and L in village, then turn R to continue past lake Nuntași and climb gently through **Istria** (128.5km, 23m) (camping). Road descends to **Sinoe** (137km, 12m) then climbs through **Mihai Viteazu** (139.5km, 57m) (refreshments, station) where it crosses an uneven railway level crossing. Turn R at T-junction (Dn22), climbing to summit at 96m and descending to **Baia** (149km, 12m) (accommodation, refreshments, station).

Just before end of village turn R (sp Ceamurila de Jos), cross railway then follow country road to T-junction and turn R (Dj222) through **Ceamurila de Jos** (154.5km, 6m) (station). Continue through **Lunca** (158km, 6m) (accommodation, refreshments) and **Vișina** (164.5km, 11m) into **Jurilovca** (167km, 21m) (accommodation, refreshments, camping).

About 40 per cent of the population of **Jurilovca** (pop. 3700) are Lipovan 'Old Believers' who fled Russia to avoid religious persecution in the early 19th century and who still speak archaic Russian. The town has developed into the largest fishing community in the Danube Delta.

In middle of village, turn L at road junction (Str 6 Marchi) and follow tree-lined road over small ridge and down into **Sălcioara** (172km, 8m). Beyond village, road undulates over a series of ridges with extensive views of Danube Delta and **Cetatea Heracleea** castle to reach **Enisala** (183.5km, 21m) (accommodation).

Cetatea Heracleea, a 12th-century medieval fortress, was built by the Byzantines on a limestone bluff overlooking Enisala. Expanded by the Genoese in the 14th century, it fell to the Ottoman Turks (1421) and was abandoned after 1651. The impressive ruins have been partly reconstructed.

Well preserved Heracleea Byzantine castle overlooks the Danube Delta near Enisala

Tulcea has a busy quayside where boats leave for Delta destinations

Turn R at beginning of village (sp Tulcea Dj222). Cross Enisala canal, which connects lake Babadag with lake Razim and enter Danube Delta nature reserve. Continue to **Sarichioi** (192km, 28m) (accommodation, refreshments, camping). Turn R and L in village continuing through **Sabangia** (196.5km, 4m) to reach **Agighiol** (203km, 7m).

> **Agighiol** is the site of a fifth-century BC Greco-Dacian tomb, in which a silver helmet was discovered. This is now in the National History museum in Bucharest. The stony hillsides south-west of the village are a protected landscape where one can find large numbers of fossils.

After village, tree-lined road climbs steadily for 10km through open fields to summit at 135m, then descends towards Tulcea. At entry to city, take third exit at roundabout (Str Mahmudiei, cobbles) and climb over one of Tulcea's seven hills. Turn R at T-junction by Tulcea 0km marker (Str Păcii) to reach roundabout with fountain in centre. Turn L (Str Isaccei) parallel with Danube promenade and at next roundabout turn R to reach station and boat quays in **Tulcea** (223km, 3m) (accommodation, refreshments, tourist office, cycle shop, station). For descriptions of Tulcea and the Danube Delta, see Stages 32 and 32A.

Clockwise from top: Archaeological museum and statue of Roman poet Ovid in Constanța's Piața Ovidiu; The House of Lions in Constanța was formerly a masonic temple; Constanța Orthodox cathedral; Jurilovca has a sign in Russian because 40 per cent of its inhabitants are Russian 'Old Believers'

APPENDIX A
Facilities summary

	Distance (km)	Cum. distance (km)	Altitude (m)	Accommodation	Meals	Camping	Tourist office	Cycle shop	Station
Stage 1									
Budapest			104	x	x	x	x	x	x
Gubacs	9.5	9.5	102	x	x			x	x
Soroksár	3.5	13	100	x	x				x
Dunaharaszti	5	18	100	x	x				x
Szigetszentmiklós	5	23	96	x	x	x		x	x
Szigetcsep	11.5	34.5	100		x				x
Szigetszentmarton	4.5	39	100	x	x	x			x
Ráckeve	8	47	100	x	x	x	x	x	x
Stage 2									
Dömsöd	9.5	56.5	99	x	x	x			
Szentgyörgypuszta	9	65.5	95	x	x				
Tass (alt route)			99	x	x				
Szalkszentmárton (alt route)			94	x	x				
Dunavecse	15	80.5	98	x	x				
Dunaegyháza	11.5	92	104		x				
Petőfitelep	2	94	99	x	x				
Dunaföldvár (4km o/r)			101	x	x	x	x	x	
Solt	3.5	97.5	97	x	x				
Stage 3									
Harta	13	110.5	94	x	x	x			
Dunapataj	8.5	119	94	x	x				
Foktő	19	138	93		x				
Kalocsa (4km o/r)			95	x	x		x	x	

	Distance (km)	Cum. distance (km)	Altitude (m)	Accommodation	Meals	Camping	Tourist office	Cycle shop	Station
Stage 4									
Meszesen	5	143	91		x	x			
Fajsz	9.5	152.5	88		x				
Érsekcsanád	19.5	172	89		x				
Baja	10.5	182.5	96	x	x	x	x	x	x
Stage 5									
Dunafalva	20	202.5	85	x	x	x			
Újmohács	13.5	216	85		x	x			
Mohács	0.5	216.5	86	x	x		x	x	x
Stage 6									
Gajić	30	246.5	84	x					
Draž	1.5	248	83	x	x				
Batina	5	253	85	x	x				
Zmajevac	5.5	258.5	87	x					
Suza	3	261.5	89	x	x	x			
Podunavlje	20.5	282	81	x					
Kopačevo	5	287	83	x	x				
Bilje	3	290	84	x	x		x		
Osijek	7.5	297.5	79	x	x		x	x	x
Stage 7									
Sarvaš	13	310.5	90						x
Bijelo Brdo	3	313.5	90	x	x				x
Dalj	10	323.5	83	x	x				x
Borovo Naselje	14	337.5	85	x	x				x
Vukovar	4.5	342	81	x	x		x	x	x
Stage 8									
Sotin	10	352	109		x				
Opatovac	7.5	359.5	84	x	x				

	Distance (km)	Cum. distance (km)	Altitude (m)	Accommodation	Meals	Camping	Tourist office	Cycle shop	Station
Šarengrad	10	369.5	81	x	x	x			
Ilok	7.5	377	132	x	x			x	x
Bačka Palanka	5.5	382.5	81	x	x	x		x	x
Stage 9									
Begeč	22	404.5	78	x					
Futog	6	410.5	79	x	x			x	x
Veternik	6	416.5	76	x	x				
Novi Sad	9.5	426	79	x	x			x	x	x
Stage 10									
Petrovaradin	2.5	428.5	79	x	x				x
Sremski Karlovci	6.5	435	86	x	x		x		x
Čortanovci	11	446	158	x		x			
Beška	6.5	452.5	120	x	x				x
Krčedin	5	457.5	112		x				
Novi Slankamen	9.5	467	146		x				
Stari Slankamen (1.5km o/r)			83	x	x				
Stage 11									
Surduk	9	476	105		x				
Belegiš	6	482	97		x				
Stari Banovci	6	488	75		x				
Banovci Dunav	2	490	89	x	x				
Novi Banovci	1	491	89	x	x				
Batajnica	6	497	77	x	x			x	x
Zemun	13	510	78	x	x	x		x	x
Novi Beograd	2.5	512.5	75	x	x			x	x
Belgrade	7.5	520	82	x	x		x	x	x

	Distance (km)	Cum. distance (km)	Altitude (m)	Accommodation	Meals	Camping	Tourist office	Cycle shop	Station
Stage 12									
Pančevo	17	537	76	x	x		x	x	x
Starčevo	9.5	546.5	74		x				
Banatski Brestovac (alt route)			76			x			
Skorenovac (alt route)			74	x	x				
Jabukov Cvet	21	567.5	68			x			
Kovin	19.5	587	70	x	x		x	x	
Stage 13									
Manastirska Rampa	5.5	592.5	68	x	x				
Raj	6.5	599	69		x				
Gaj (alt route)			79	x	x				
Šumarak (alt route)			99	x					
Dubovac	11.5	610.5	74	x	x	x			
Stara Palanka	16	626.5	69	x	x				
Stage 14									
Ram	0	626.5	69		x				
Zatonje	7	633.5	84		x				
Beli Bagrem	8	641.5	70	x	x	x			
Veliko Gradište	3.5	645	71		x		x		
Požeženo	5	650	68		x				
Vinci	6.5	656.5	71	x	x				
Golubac	8	664.5	73	x	x		x	x	
Stage 15									
Ridan	5	669.5	82	x	x				
Brnjica	7	676.5	72		x				
Čezava	6	682.5	86			x			
Dobra	6	688.5	71	x	x				

	Distance (km)	Cum. distance (km)	Altitude (m)	Accommodation	Meals	Camping	Tourist office	Cycle shop	Station
Lepenski vir	16	704.5	120		x				
Stara Oreškovica	14	718.5	66	x	x	x			
Donji Milanovac	3	721.5	72	x	x		x	x	
Stage 16									
Malo Golubinje	15	736.5	72	x					
Tekija	25	761.5	76	x	x	x			
Novi Sip (3km o/r)			80	x	x				
Gura Văii	3.5	778	74						x
Schela Cladovei	7	785	74	x	x				
Drobeta-Turnu Severin	3.5	788.5	70	x	x			x	x
Stage 17									
Şimian	7	795.5	59	x	x				
Hinova	9.5	805	45	x	x				
Gruia	55	860	94	x	x				
Stage 18									
Cetate	37.5	897.5	85	x	x				
Maglavit	10	907.5	75						x
Golenţi	5	912.5	68		x				x
Basarabi	4	916.5	63	x	x				
Calafat	6	922.5	54	x	x			x	x
Stage 19									
Poiana Mare	14.5	937	39		x				
Zăval	68.5	1005.5	47	x	x	x			
Bechet	13	1018.5	40	x	x				
Stage 20									
Corabia	45.5	1064	47	x	x			x	x
Stage 21									
Islaz	20.5	1084.5	31	x	x				

	Distance (km)	Cum. distance (km)	Altitude (m)	Accommodation	Meals	Camping	Tourist office	Cycle shop	Station
Turnu Măgurele	10	1094.5	36	x	x			x	
Stage 22									
Traian	12	1106.5	35		x				
Zimnicea	45	1151.5	34	x	x			x	
Stage 23									
Giurgiu	60	1211.5	24	x	x		x	x	x
Stage 24									
Giurgiu Nord	3.5	1215	21	x	x				x
Daia	7.5	1222.5	30	x	x				
Greaca	36.5	1259	72	x	x				
Oltenița	28.5	1287.5	18	x	x				x
Stage 25									
Mânăstirea	30	1317.5	17		x				
Călărași	40	1357.5	21	x	x			x	x
Stage 26									
Chiciu	9	1366.5	14	x	x				
Silistra (Bulgaria)	2	1368.5	19	x	x			x	x
Ostrov	5.5	1374	28	x	x				
Lipnița	25	1399	103	x					
Băneasa	9.5	1408.5	96	x	x		x		
Negureni	7	1415.5	62	x	x				
Ion Corvin	7	1422.5	70	x	x				
Stage 27									
Cernavodă	40.5	1463	17	x	x		x		x
Stage 28									
Seimenii Mici	6	1469	18	x	x				
Capidava	16.5	1485.5	18	x	x	x			
Hârșova	30.5	1516	32	x	x				

	Distance (km)	Cum. distance (km)	Altitude (m)	Accommodation	Meals	Camping	Tourist office	Cycle shop	Station
Stage 29									
Măcin	88	1604	22	x	x		x		
Stage 30									
Brăila (2.5km o/r)			21	x	x	x	x	x	x
Galați	30	1634	7	x	x		x	x	x
Stage 31									
Luncavița	25	1659	18	x	x				
Isaccea	17	1676	11	x	x				
Stage 31A									
Reni (alt route)	24	(24)	15	x	x	x			
Isaccea (alt route)	28	(52)	11	x	x				
Stage 32									
Mineri	29	1705	26	x	x				
Tulcea	7	1712	3	x	x		x	x	x
Stage 32A									
Crişan (excursion)	49.5	(49.5)	0	x	x				
Sulina (excursion)	21.5	(71)	0	x	x				

APPENDIX B

Tourist information offices

Stage 1
Budapest (no accommodation details)
Városháza park, Károly körút
1052
+36 30 955 0398
www.budapestinfo.hu

Ráckeve
Eőtvős út 1
2300
+36 24 429 747
www.tourinformrackeve.hu

Stage 2
Dunafoldvár
Rátkai köz 2
7020
+36 75 541 083
www.dunafoldvar.hu

Stage 3
Kalocsa
Szent István király utca 35
6300
+36 30 467 8690
www.turizmuskalocsa.hu

Stage 4
Baja
Szentháromság tér 11
6500
+36 79 420 792
www.csodalatosbaja.hu

Stage 5
Mohács
Szent János utca 5
7700
+36 69 341 659
www.mohacs.hu

Stage 6
Bilje
Krala Zvonmira 10
31327
+385 99 733 2001
www.tzo-bilje.hr

Osijek (Tvrđa)
Trg sv Trojstva 5
31000
+385 31 210 120
www.tzosijek.hr

Osijek (Gornji Grad)
Županijska ul 2
31000
+385 31 203 755
www.tzosijek.hr

Stage 7
Vukovar
JJ Strossmayera 15
32000
+385 32 442 889
www.turizamvukovar.hr

Stage 8
Ilok
Trg Nikole Iločkog 2
32236
+385 32 590 020
www.turizamilok.hr

Bačka Palanka
Veselin Masleše 8
21400
+381 21 750 105
www.toobap.rs

Stage 9
Novi Sad
Trg slobode 3
21001
+381 21 661 7343
www.novisad.travel.rs

Stage 10
Sremski Karlovci
Patrijarha Rajačića 1
21205
+381 21 882 127
www.karlovci.org.rs

Indija
Cara Dušána 1
22320
+381 22 510 970
www.indjijatravel.rs

Stage 11
Belgrade
Knez Mihailova 56
11000
+381 11 263 5622
www.tob.rs

Stage 12
Pančevo
Vojvode Petra Bojovića 2
26101
+381 13 333 399
www.visitpancevo.rs

Kovin
Cara Lazara 86b
26220
+381 13 745 860
www.turizamkovin.rs

Stage 13
Bela Crkva
Proleterska 2
26340
+381 13 851 777
www.belacrkvato.org

Stage 14
Veliko Gradište
Vojvode Putnika 2
12220
+381 12 663 179
www.tovg.org

Golubac
Gorana Tošića Mačka 1
12223
+381 12 638 614
www.togolubac.rs

Stage 15
Donji Milanovac
Kralja Petra 14
19220
+381 30 591 400
www.toom.rs

Stage 23
Giurgiu
Parcul Mihai Viteazui
+40 346 566 955

Stage 26
Băneasa
Str Trandafirilor 57
+40 241 851 018

Stage 27
Cernavodă
Str Crişan 1
+40 241 487 175

Stage 29
Macin
Str Brăilei 9B
+40 787 544 050
www.turism-macin.ro

Stage 30
Brăila
Str Edmond Nicolau 4A
+40 786 478 494
www.cniptbraila.ro

Stage 32
Tulcea
Str Gloriei 2
+40 240 519 055

Stage 27–32 variant
Murfatlar
Calea Bucureşti 3B
+40 341 451 855

Constanţa (website only)
www.primaria-constanta.ro/turism

APPENDIX C
Useful contacts

Transportation
Eurostar
www.eurostar.com (tickets and schedules)
travelservices@eurostar.com (cycle reservations)

SNCF (French railways)
www.sncf-connect.com

Deutsche Bahn (German railways)
+49 30 31 168 2904 (in English)
+49 30 29 60 (in German)
www.bahn.com

NS (Dutch railways)
+31 30 751 51 55
www.ns.nl

ÖBB (Austrian railways)
+43 05 1717
www.oebb.at

CFR (Romanian railways)
www.cfrcalatori.ro

'The man in seat 61' rail travel information
www.seat61.com

P & O (Harwich–Hoek ferry)
0871 664 2121 (UK)
+44 130 486 3000 (outside UK)
+31 20 200 8333 (NL)
www.poferries.com

Stena Line (Hull–Rotterdam ferry)
+44 844 770 7070
www.stenaline.co.uk

DFDS (Newcastle–Ijmuiden ferry)
+44 871 574 7235
www.dfds.com

Excess Baggage Company
(bike boxes at London airports)
www.left-baggage.co.uk

Wiggle
(polythene bike bags)
www.wiggle.co.uk

Danube Delta Ferries
Str Portului 26
Tulcea
+40 240 511 528
www.navromdelta.ro

Accommodation
Hostelling International (YHA)
(official youth hostel reservations)
www.hihostels.com

Independent hostels
(independent and backpacker hostel listings)
www.hostelbookers.com
www.hostelworld.com

Tourist Organisation of Serbia (TOS)
(accommodation listings in Serbia)
www.srbija.travel/en/accommodation

National tourist information in Romania
(accommodation listings in Romania)
www.romania.travel.com

Maps and guides

European Cycling Federation
(downloadable route map)
www.en.eurovelo.com/ev6

Huber Kartographie
www.cartography-huber.com

Open Street Maps
(online mapping)
www.openstreetmap.org

Stanfords
7 Mercer Walk
London WC2H 9FA
+44 207 836 1321
sales@stanfords.co.uk
www.stanfords.co.uk

The Map Shop
15 High St
Upton upon Severn, Worcs
WR8 0HJ
+44 800 085 4080 or +44 168 459
3146
themapshop@btinternet.com
www.themapshop.co.uk

Cycling organisations

Cycling UK
(formerly Cyclist's Touring Club)
+44 148 323 8301 (membership)
+44 333 003 0046 (insurance)
www.cyclinguk.org

APPENDIX D
Language glossary

English	Hungarian	Croatian [Serbian Cyrillic]	Romanian
barrier	sorompó	prepreka [препрека]	barieră
bridge	hid	most [мост]	pod
bicycle	kerékpár/bicikli]	bicikl [бицикл]	bicicletă
castle	kastély/var	dvorac [дворац]	castel
cathedral	katedrális	katedrala [катедрала]	catedrală
church	templom	crkva [црква]	biserică
cycle track	kerékpárút	biciklistička staža [бициклистичке стазе]	pista de bicicletă
cyclist	kerékpáros	biciklista [бициклистичка]	cyclist
dam	gát	brana [брана]	baraj
diversion	kerülő út	diverzija [диверэија]	deviere
dyke	védőgát	nasip [насип]	dig/barej
ferry	komp/rév	trajekt [трајект]	bac
field	mezzo	polje [поље]	camp
floods	árviz	poplava [поплава]	inundatii
forest/woods	erdő	šuma [шума]	pădure
fort	erőd	tvrđava [тврђава]	cetate
guest house	panzió	pansion [пансион]	pensiune
monastery	kolostor	manastir [манастир]	mănăstirea
monument	műemlék	spomenik [споменик]	monument
motorway	autópálya	autocesta [аутоцеста]	autostradă
no entry	behajtani tilos	zabranjen ulaz [забрањен улаз]	acces interzis
one-way street	egyirányú utca	jednosmjerna ulica [једносмерна улица]	sens unic
puncture	defect	defect [дефект]	pană
railway	vasút	željeznica [железница]	cale ferată
river	folyó	rijeka [река]	râu
riverbank	folyópart	obala [обала]	malul raului
road closed	útlezárás	zatvorena česta [затворена]	drum închis
station	állomás	stanica [станица]	gară
tourist information office	információs iroda	turistički ured [туристички биро]	informaţii turistice
town hall	városháza	gradska vijećnica [градска већница]	primărie
youth hostel	hostel/ifjúsági szálló	hostel [хостел]	youth hostel

APPENDIX E

Serbian Cyrillic alphabet

Serb Cyrillic		Croat Latin		English
u/c	l/c	u/c	l/c	phonetic
А	а	A	a	a
Б	б	B	b	Be
В	в	V	v	Ve
Г	г	G	g	Ge
Д	д	D	d	De
Ђ	ђ	Đ	đ	Dje
Е	е	E	e	e
Ж	ж	Ž	ž	Zhe
З	з	Z	z	Ze
И	и	I	i	i
J	j	J	j	Je
К	к	K	k	Ka
Л	л	L	l	eL
Љ	љ	LJ	lj	Lje
М	м	M	m	eM
Н	н	N	n	eN
Њ	њ	NJ	nj	Nje
О	о	O	o	o
П	п	P	p	Pe
Р	р	R	r	eR
С	с	S	s	eS
Т	т	T	t	Te
Ћ	ћ	Ć	ć	Tshe
У	у	U	u	u
Ф	ф	F	f	eF
Х	х	H	h	Kha
Ц	ц	C	c	Tse
Ч	ч	Č	č	Che
Џ	џ	DŽ	dž	Dzhe
Ш	ш	Š	š	Sha

DOWNLOAD THE GPX FILES

All the routes in this guide are available for download from:

www.cicerone.co.uk/1189/GPX

as standard format GPX files. You should be able to load them into most online GPX systems and mobile devices, whether GPS or smartphone. You may need to convert the file into your preferred format using a conversion programme such as gpsvisualizer.com or one of the many other such websites and programmes.

When you follow this link, you will be asked for your email address and where you purchased the guidebook, and have the option to subscribe to the Cicerone e-newsletter.

www.cicerone.co.uk

NOTES

NOTES

NOTES

LISTING OF CICERONE GUIDES

BRITISH ISLES CHALLENGES, COLLECTIONS AND ACTIVITIES

Cycling Land's End to John o' Groats
Great Walks on the England
    Coast Path
The Big Rounds
The Book of the Bivvy
The Book of the Bothy
The Mountains of England & Wales:
    Vol 1 Wales
    Vol 2 England
The National Trails
Walking the End to End Trail

SHORT WALKS SERIES

Short Walks Hadrian's Wall
Short Walks in Arnside
    and Silverdale
Short Walks in Dumfries
    and Galloway
Short Walks in Nidderdale
Short Walks in the Lake District:
    Windermere Ambleside
    and Grasmere
Short Walks in the Surrey Hills
Short Walks Lake District – Coniston
    and Langdale
Short Walks on the Malvern Hills
Short Walks Winchester

SCOTLAND

Ben Nevis and Glen Coe
Cycle Touring in Northern Scotland
Cycling in the Hebrides
Cycling the North Coast 500
Great Mountain Days in Scotland
Mountain Biking in Southern and
    Central Scotland
Mountain Biking in West and North
    West Scotland
Not the West Highland Way
    Scotland
Scotland's Best Small Mountains
Scotland's Mountain Ridges
Scottish Wild Country Backpacking
Skye's Cuillin Ridge Traverse
The Borders Abbeys Way
The Great Glen Way
The Great Glen Way Map Booklet
The Hebridean Way
The Hebrides
The Isle of Mull
The Isle of Skye
The Skye Trail
The Southern Upland Way
The West Highland Way
The West Highland Way
    Map Booklet
Walking Ben Lawers, Rannoch
    and Atholl
Walking in the Cairngorms

Walking in the Pentland Hills
Walking in the Scottish Borders
Walking in the Southern Uplands
Walking in Torridon, Fisherfield,
    Fannichs and An Teallach
Walking Loch Lomond and
    the Trossachs
Walking on Arran
Walking on Harris and Lewis
Walking on Jura, Islay and Colonsay
Walking on Rum and the Small Isles
Walking on the Orkney and
    Shetland Isles
Walking on Uist and Barra
Walking the Cape Wrath Trail
Walking the Corbetts
    Vol 1 South of the Great Glen
    Vol 2 North of the Great Glen
Walking the Galloway Hills
Walking the John o' Groats Trail
Walking the Munros
    Vol 1 – Southern, Central and
    Western Highlands
    Vol 2 – Northern Highlands and
    the Cairngorms
Winter Climbs in the Cairngorms
Winter Climbs: Ben Nevis and
    Glen Coe

NORTHERN ENGLAND ROUTES

Cycling the Reivers Route
Cycling the Way of the Roses
Hadrian's Cycleway
Hadrian's Wall Path
Hadrian's Wall Path Map Booklet
The Coast to Coast Cycle Route
The Coast to Coast Walk
The Coast to Coast Walk
    Map Booklet
The Pennine Way
The Pennine Way Map Booklet
Walking the Dales Way
Walking the Dales Way Map Booklet

NORTH-EAST ENGLAND, YORKSHIRE DALES AND PENNINES

Cycling in the Yorkshire Dales
Great Mountain Days in
    the Pennines
Mountain Biking in the
    Yorkshire Dales
The Cleveland Way and the
    Yorkshire Wolds Way
The Cleveland Way Map Booklet
The North York Moors
Trail and Fell Running in the
    Yorkshire Dales
Walking in County Durham
Walking in Northumberland
Walking in the North Pennines

Walking in the Yorkshire Dales:
    North and East
Walking in the Yorkshire Dales:
    South and West
Walking St Cuthbert's Way
Walking St Oswald's Way and
    Northumberland Coast Path

NORTH-WEST ENGLAND AND THE ISLE OF MAN

Cycling the Pennine Bridleway
Isle of Man Coastal Path
The Lancashire Cycleway
The Lune Valley and Howgills
Walking in Cumbria's Eden Valley
Walking in Lancashire
Walking in the Forest of Bowland
    and Pendle
Walking on the Isle of Man
Walking on the West Pennine Moors
Walking the Ribble Way
Walks in Silverdale and Arnside

LAKE DISTRICT

Bikepacking in the Lake District
Cycling in the Lake District
Great Mountain Days in the
    Lake District
Joss Naylor's Lakes, Meres and
    Waters of the Lake District
Lake District Winter Climbs
Lake District: High Level and Fell
    Walks
Lake District: Low Level and Lake
    Walks
Mountain Biking in the Lake District
Outdoor Adventures with Children –
    Lake District
Scrambles in the Lake District –
    North
Scrambles in the Lake District –
    South
Trail and Fell Running in the
    Lake District
Walking The Cumbria Way
Walking the Lake District Fells:
    Borrowdale
    Buttermere
    Coniston
    Keswick
    Langdale
    Mardale and the Far East
    Patterdale
    Wasdale
Walking the Tour of the Lake District

DERBYSHIRE, PEAK DISTRICT AND MIDLANDS

Cycling in the Peak District
Dark Peak Walks
Scrambles in the Dark Peak
Walking in Derbyshire

Walking in the Peak District –
    White Peak East
Walking in the Peak District –
    White Peak West

SOUTHERN ENGLAND

20 Classic Sportive Rides:
    In South East England
    In South West England
Cycling in the Cotswolds
Mountain Biking on the
    North Downs
Mountain Biking on the
    South Downs
Suffolk Coast and Heath Walks
The Cotswold Way
The Cotswold Way Map Booklet
The Kennet and Avon Canal
The Lea Valley Walk
The North Downs Way
The North Downs Way Map Booklet
The Peddars Way and Norfolk
    Coast Path
The Pilgrims' Way
The Ridgeway National Trail
The Ridgeway National Trail
    Map Booklet
The South Downs Way
The South Downs Way Map Booklet
The Thames Path
The Thames Path Map Booklet
The Two Moors Way
Two Moors Way Map Booklet
Walking Hampshire's Test Way
Walking in Cornwall
Walking in Essex
Walking in Kent
Walking in London
Walking in Norfolk
Walking in the Chilterns
Walking in the Cotswolds
Walking in the Isles of Scilly
Walking in the New Forest
Walking in the North Wessex Downs
Walking on Dartmoor
Walking on Guernsey
Walking on Jersey
Walking on the Isle of Wight
Walking the Dartmoor Way
Walking the Jurassic Coast
Walking the South West Coast Path
Walking the South West Coast Path
    Map Booklets:
    Vol 1: Minehead to St Ives
    Vol 2: St Ives to Plymouth
    Vol 3: Plymouth to Poole
Walks in the South Downs
    National Park

WALES AND WELSH BORDERS

Cycle Touring in Wales
Cycling Lon Las Cymru
Great Mountain Days in Snowdonia

Hillwalking in Shropshire
Mountain Walking in Snowdonia
Offa's Dyke Path
Offa's Dyke Path Map Booklet
Ridges of Snowdonia
Scrambles in Snowdonia
Snowdonia –
    30 Low-level and Easy Walks:
    – North
    – South
The Cambrian Way
The Pembrokeshire Coast Path
The Snowdonia Way
The Wye Valley Walk
Walking in Carmarthenshire
Walking in Pembrokeshire
Walking in the Brecon Beacons
Walking in the Forest of Dean
Walking in the Wye Valley
Walking on Gower
Walking the Severn Way
Walking the Shropshire Way
Walking the Wales Coast Path

INTERNATIONAL CHALLENGES, COLLECTIONS AND ACTIVITIES

Europe's High Points
Walking the Via Francigena
    Pilgrim Route – Part 1

AFRICA

Kilimanjaro
Walking in the Drakensberg
Walks and Scrambles in the
    Moroccan Anti-Atlas

ALPS CROSS-BORDER ROUTES

100 Hut Walks in the Alps
Alpine Ski Mountaineering
    Vol 1 – Western Alps
The Karnischer Hohenweg
The Tour of the Bernina
Trail Running – Chamonix and the
    Mont Blanc region
Trekking Chamonix to Zermatt
Trekking in the Alps
Trekking in the Silvretta and
    Ratikon Alps
Trekking Munich to Venice
Trekking the Tour of Mont Blanc
Walking in the Alps

PYRENEES AND FRANCE/SPAIN CROSS-BORDER ROUTES

Shorter Treks in the Pyrenees
The GR11 Trail
The Pyrenean Haute Route
The Pyrenees
Walks and Climbs in the Pyrenees

AUSTRIA

Innsbruck Mountain Adventures
Trekking Austria's Adlerweg

Trekking in Austria's Hohe Tauern
Trekking in Austria's Zillertal Alps
Trekking in the Stubai Alps
Walking in Austria
Walking in the Salzkammergut:
    the Austrian Lake District

EASTERN EUROPE

The Danube Cycleway Vol 2
The Elbe Cycle Route
The High Tatras
The Mountains of Romania
Walking in Hungary

FRANCE, BELGIUM AND LUXEMBOURG

Camino de Santiago – Via Podiensis
Chamonix Mountain Adventures
Cycle Touring in France
Cycling London to Paris
Cycling the Canal de la Garonne
Cycling the Canal du Midi
Cycling the Route des Grandes Alpes
Mont Blanc Walks
Mountain Adventures in
    the Maurienne
Short Treks on Corsica
The GR5 Trail
The GR5 Trail – Benelux
    and Lorraine
The GR5 Trail – Vosges and Jura
The Grand Traverse of the
    Massif Central
The Moselle Cycle Route
The River Loire Cycle Route
The River Rhone Cycle Route
Trekking in the Vanoise
Trekking the Cathar Way
Trekking the GR10
Trekking the GR20 Corsica
Trekking the Robert Louis
    Stevenson Trail
Via Ferratas of the French Alps
Walking in Provence – East
Walking in Provence – West
Walking in the Ardennes
Walking in the Auvergne
Walking in the Brianconnais
Walking in the Dordogne
Walking in the Haute Savoie: North
Walking in the Haute Savoie: South
Walking on Corsica
Walking the Brittany Coast Path

GERMANY

Hiking and Cycling in the
    Black Forest
The Danube Cycleway Vol 1
The Rhine Cycle Route
The Westweg
Walking in the Bavarian Alps

For full information on all our
guides, books and eBooks,
visit our website:
www.cicerone.co.uk

CICERONE

Trust Cicerone to guide your next adventure,
wherever it may be around the world...

Discover guides for hiking, mountain walking, backpacking,
trekking, trail running, cycling and mountain biking, ski touring,
climbing and scrambling in Britain, Europe and worldwide.

Connect with Cicerone online and find inspiration.

- buy books and ebooks
- articles, advice and trip reports
- podcasts and live events
- GPX files and updates
- regular newsletter

cicerone.co.uk